Breed Lover's Guide™

HAVANESE

A Practical Guide for the Havanese Lover

WITHDRAWN

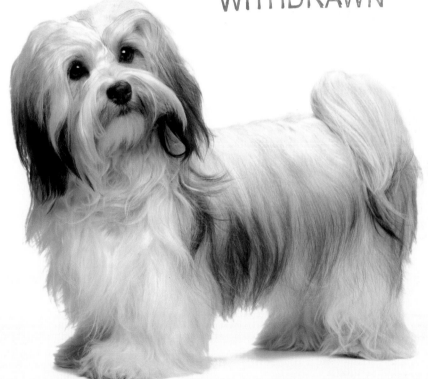

Patricia B. McRae, Ph.D.

tfh

Havanese

Project Team
Editor: Mary E. Grangeia
Copy Editor: Joann Woy
Indexer: Sonja Armstrong
Design: Patricia Escabi

TFH Publications, Inc.®
One TFH Plaza
Third and Union Avenues
Neptune City, NJ 07753

TFH Publications®
President/CEO: Glen S. Axelrod
Executive Vice President: Mark E. Johnson
Publisher: Christopher T. Reggio
Production Manager: Kathy Bontz

Printed and bound in China
12 13 14 15 16   1 3 5 7 9 8 6 4 2

Library of Congress Cataloging-in-Publication Data
McRae, Patricia B.
  Havanese / Patricia McRae.
      p. cm.
  Includes index.
  ISBN 978-0-7938-4183-7 (alk. paper)
  1. Havanese dog. I. Title.
  SF429.H37M37 2012
  636.76--dc23

                              2011031436

The Leader In Responsible Animal Care For Over 50 Years!®
www.tfh.com

Table of Contents

Chapter 1

History of
the Havanese

As you stand on a corner in Havana, you may see him peeking through the bars of a balcony, frolicking in the park with his people, or barking from the front door of his home at those he knows and doesn't know. This charming little white dog, saucy and boisterous, is known to most Cubans as a Maltese, but he is actually a Bichon Habanero, or Toy Havanese. Ask any owner of a Havanese why it takes so long to finish a morning walk and she will tell you it's because she is frequently stopped along the way and asked: "What kind of dog are you walking? A *hava-knees*, as in my knee?" After meeting one, most people want to find out more about this cheerful, happy, and incredibly intelligent toy dog.

Bichon Family of Dogs

Officially, the Havanese is one of a number of breeds that comprise the Bichon family of dogs: Bichon Maltese, Bichon Frise, Bichon Bolognese, Lowchen, Bichon Havanese, the Russian Tsvetnaya Bolonka, and the Coton de Tulear. "Bichon" is a French word referring to any small, long-haired dog. Some believe "Bichon" may be derived from the word "barbichon," which is related to "barbet," a generic name for a dog with a long, curly, woolly coat. What most of these dogs have in common is that they are small, white, curly-coated, and lacking distinctive breed characteristics. Identifiable breed characteristics are achieved only through carefully planned breeding programs. The early Bichon was an ancient type of French water spaniel, derived from the Poodle, from which all Bichons are thought to have evolved. [*Bichon Havanese* by Zoila Portuondo]. The breed is also believed to share lineage with the Maltese, the Poodle, and a dog of the Canary Islands later known as the Bichon Frise.

Some fanciers believe that the small, white, silky-coated dogs called Blanquitos de la Habana (Little White Dogs of Havana) or Perros de Seda de la Habana (Havanese Silk Dogs) were not Havanese as we know them today, but were a precursor of the breeding of the Havanese.and the Blanquito. The Blanquito eventually died off by the late 1700s, probably because of numerous breeding programs that had as their goal making the Blanquito smaller and smaller, until the dogs only averaged 3 to 6 lbs (1 to 3 kg). Breeding dogs who were too small caused a severe decline in the health of the Blanquito. At this point, the idea arose that breeding the French Poodle to the Blanquito would strengthen the breed and introduce greater color variety. This is the foundation upon which the originator of the Habanero Club de Cuba, Zoila Portuondo, bases her theory that there have been two breeds of Havanese: the first being the white-coated Blanquito, which eventually died off, and later, today's Havanese, which evolved from subsequent crossings with other breeds and developed into the dog of many splendored colors we now know.

Breed Origins: From Europe to Cuba and Back

The precise development of the Havanese breed remains shrouded in mystery. After the fall of the Roman Empire (395–476 AD) and the advance of the Dark Ages, more properly known as the European Middle Ages, most of the continent suffered widespread intellectual, economic, and political stagnation. Resources were thin, and the population struggled to survive famine and plagues. Dogs were kept for utilitarian purposes. Increased overseas exploration and trading eventually stimulated a recovery, and among those items traded were small

The Havanese is believed to be a descendant of breeds brought to Cuba from Europe and could also be related to the Tenerife, and ancestor of the entire Bichon family of dogs.

white dogs brought to Europe by sea captains on their journeys to and from other continents. The smaller of these dogs, referred to as *curs*, hunted and killed plague-carrying vermin on ships and docks. Although the bubonic plague still festered in Europe during this time, researchers speculate that in those places where these small dogs lived and hunted, rats were kept in check; hence, the dogs helped to stem the spread of disease. In addition to being prized for this purpose, some of these little dogs gained the favor of elites and nobility, which led to more controlled breeding and to their increased value over time.

Most researchers also note that, during the Spanish Empire (1492–1848), a small, white, silky-coated dog roamed the Mediterranean coast and was variously identified as the Little Silk Dog, Melita, or Caniche. Small, raggedy, white and colored dogs, believed to be related to these Melita or Caniche dogs, were also discovered living on the Canary Islands, which included the Island of Tenerife.

During the period ushering in the Renaissance, European monarchs wielded enormous power over their trading ships, dictating which ones could sail, where they would ship, and what they could carry. The Island of Tenerife, one of the Canary Islands discovered by Columbus, was the only island permitted shipping trade by the Kingdom of Spain. Cargo exported to and from the island included the small white dogs, later called the Tenerife Dog or Bichon Tenerife. Ancestors of the Havanese were most likely brought to Cuba aboard trade ships sailing from Tenerife. Because Cuban trade was highly restricted by the Spanish, these little dogs developed in Cuba without much outside influence, eventually finding their way into the homes of Cuban aristocracy and becoming the national dog and its only native breed. As colonial Cuba developed, so did the popularity of the "Havanese Silk Dog," which became trendy in Europe by the mid-eighteenth century. The growing popularity of these little white toy dogs among English nobility increased trade in them exponentially, leading to their eventual desirability all over Europe.

By the nineteenth century, the Bichon Havanese began to emerge as a distinct breed in its own right. Preferred not only as the family pet of Cuba's colonial aristocracy, this toy dog was also quite sought after by European monarchs, such as Queen Victoria, who owned two, and celebrities, like author Charles Dickens, who obtained one for his children. So treasured were the pets of the English royal family that a line item credit for them of 100,000 gold crowns became part of the annual budget. Later, Havanese began to appear in traveling circuses, showing off their trainability in the amount of tricks they performed, and furthering their reputation and desirability among the general population.

At the Paris Dog Show of 1863, 850 to 900 dogs were exhibited. It is thought that this was the first dog show in which the Havanese took its place among other dogs identified as members of the Bichon family.

After World War II (WWII), these small white dogs decreased in popularity as their aristocratic owners died off and/or migrated to Europe and the United States in the wake of the Cuban Revolution in 1959.

Havanese in the United States

When Cubans fled to the United States to avoid the political upheaval of the 1959 Revolution, most were not able to take their Havanese with them. The few individuals who did escape with their dogs soon introduced American breeders to this rare and charming breed.

Dorothy and Burt Goodale, breeders and exhibitors of Afghan Hounds and Irish Setters, had long heard rumors about the "little white Cuban dog," and they began tracking down Havanese between 1975 and 1979. They were able to buy 11 dogs from

Havanese first arrived in the United States in the 1970s, brought by expatriated Cubans who fled the political upheaval in their homeland. The breed was officially recognized by the American Kennel Club in 1996.

the Fantasio and Perez families, who had emigrated to Costa Rica. Later, in a search for more Havanese, Dorothy put an ad in several Florida newspapers. She received one reply from Senor Ezekiel Barba, who was on his way to Arizona to live with his daughter and could not take his six dogs with him. These seventeen Goodale Havanese became the core foundation of the breed in the United States.

Dorothy and Burt worked with friends to establish solid breeding programs. Foundation Havanese kennels included not only Dorothy's Havana Doll House, but also Arlene Gaglione's Ti-Ara Havanese, Mary Money's SRR, Sadie Stromberg's Mendoza Havanese, Mark Kolbe's Hallmark Havanese, Kathleen Schmidt's Katrina Havanese, Elizabeth Vargo's Destiny Havanese, and Eugene Malcolm's Setacane Havanese. In 1979, Dorothy Goodale, along with this nucleus of passionate breeders, formed the Havanese Club of America, which was recognized by the American Kennel Club (AKC) as the parent club of the breed.

Meanwhile, Europe began to rediscover the little Cuban dog as well, and exports from the United States began as early as 1981. Pillowtalk Kennel, owned by Monika and Al Moser of Germany, was the first to acquire dogs. Then Anja van Haarlem of A Maiden Effort Kennel in The Netherlands saw a photo of SSR's Mr. Sandman in a Dutch dog magazine and learned that the dog was imported from the United States by Monika Moser. Seeking her own Havanese, Anja obtained Pillowtalk Kennel's Chicita, who produced a large number of progeny and has left an admirable legacy. About this time, another champion dog, Mucho Bravo's Wild Willy, of Mucho Bravo Kennel in Germany, owned by Rene and Mirabell Woudman, would become one of the top-placing Havanese in Europe. Mucho Bravo Kennel, and its champion stud Wild Willy, also did well at reaching across the

WHAT IS A BREED CLUB?

A breed club is a nonprofit organization of dog fanciers dedicated to the preservation and betterment of a specific breed of purebred dog. Each club writes the standard for their breed and maintains their breed's stud book. The breed standard is a blueprint for the breed that describes its form and function. Each time breeders take their dogs into the show ring, they are measuring their breeding program against this standard for the breed—in other words, how close their breeding decisions come to meeting the standard for the breed. They also provide information about their breed to the public and offer educational resources to breed owners. Breed clubs may also sponsor dog shows or competitions in various dog sports, and many raise funds for research on breed-specific health issues. The Havanese Club of America (HCA) is the parent breed club for local Havanese clubs in the United States.

Atlantic to work with American Havanese breeders to improve the lines.

By the mid-1980s, the original smattering of Havanese breeding kennels in the United States, among which were Elizabeth Vargo of Destiny Havanese and Marsha Peterson of the original Elfin Havanese, increased in number.

With dedicated breeding and the acquisition of dogs from other countries, the Havanese eventually became one of the fastest growing dog breeds in the AKC.

The Modern Havanese in Cuba

In Cuba, in 1988, Cuba Ch. Puppy, a Havanese star, was born. Puppy's birth coincided with the repatriation of the breed to its native country. In 1992, the Federacíon Cinológica de Cuba (FCC) worked with the Department of Communications and Cuba's postal service to issue a series of stamps honoring dogs and requested that Puppy be used as the model for the Havanese postage stamp.

By the time Puppy was 5 years old, he was not yet a champion nor had he received any intensive show training, but he was such a fine specimen

that the Federacíon Cinológica de Cuba approached his owner, Alfredo Sanz Peraza, to allow him to compete.

It would be 1991 before the Havanese breed was listed in the Cuban registry. That year, Zoila Portuondo founded the Cuban Club of the Bichon Havanese (CCBH). The CCBH is a member of the Cuban Kennel Club (CKC) and it is, in

Kolmar's Caribbean Breeze was the first American Kennel Club HCA champion.

Ask the Expert

REGISTERED HAVANESE

Q: I just want a pet Havanese, not one to show. Why should I purchase a dog who is registered?

A: The type of dog you choose is certainly your prerogative, and you can certainly find unregistered Havanese available. But how will you know you have purchased a purebred Havanese? And how will you know he does not come from breeding lines that have shown serious genetic defects? Nothing is more heartbreaking than becoming attached to a dog and then having to return him to the breeder, or worse yet, having to put him down because of serious health problems. The AKC is the premier registry for purebred dogs in the United States and certifies their pedigrees.

Be sure to do your homework before setting off to get your Havanese puppy. The Havanese Club of America (HCA) website has a wonderful educational section for the prospective puppy buyer and for the new puppy owner at www.Havanese.org/education/puppy-buyers.

—Candace Mogavero, Faireland Havanese; Delaware AKC Judge, Show Exhibitor, Breeder.

turn, a recognized member of Federacíon Cinológica International (FCI).

In 1993, Puppy won his first championship. Havanese are growing in popularity not only in Cuba but throughout the world.

The Havanese of Today

The early 1990s saw two turning points in the evolution of the Havanese breed: in 1991, the United Kennel (UKC) officially recognized the Havanese, and in 1996, the AKC moved the Havanese from the Miscellaneous to the Toy Group class, thus bestowing formal recognition on the breed.

Despite splendid growth among the fancy during the 1990s, some dark clouds began to appear. Health testing of dogs was in its infancy, with the Orthopedic Foundation for Animals (OFA) and the Canine Eye Research Foundation (CERF) taking the lead in educating breeders and pet owners about the need to monitor breed health and breeding practices. During this period, Nancy Holmes of Nor-Ann Havanese and Elizabeth Vargo of Destiny Havanese tested their dogs for eye diseases and found they had hereditary cataracts. Needless to say, this did not endear them to their colleagues in the dog fancy, but making informed breeding decisions is critical to the maintenance and improvement of a breed, as well as to the strength of one's breeding program. To find that half of one's kennel is afflicted with cataracts is a significant and heartbreaking challenge. However, persistence and increased testing brought positive results. In 1991, it was determined that approximately 15 percent of Havanese had hereditary cataracts. Simultaneously, the development of an eye test that was affordable and mobile became available. The eye test could be performed by a canine ophthalmologist to determine the presence or absence of cataracts in breeding stock. Identification of such an affliction led to more testing and informed breeding decisions, so much so that, by 2009, according to CERF, less than 2.5 percent of Havanese develop cataracts. Additionally, Havanese rank among the top five breeds who consistently test and record their health statistics. Despite its painful consequences for some breeders, health testing in the Havanese breed is universally recognized as vital to the breed's continued success.

By 2008, the number of Havanese registered with the AKC had increased by 42 percent, and in 2009, the Havanese ranked 32nd in the number of purebred dogs registered. The number of Havanese dog clubs, including the parent Havanese Club of America, increased from 3 in 1999 to 11 by the end of 2010. The Havanese is here to stay.

Havanese are growing in popularity not only in Cuba but throughout the world.

TIMELINE

- **1492**: Christopher Columbus lands in the Americas and claims these territories as New Spain, in the name of the Kingdom of Spain. One of the islands is named Cuba Juana, after Don Juan, the infant son of Columbus' sponsors, King Ferdinand and Queen Isabella. Columbus finds that the only domesticated animals on the island of Cuba are turkeys and dogs. This is the first documented evidence of the sighting of a native dog. It is plausible that these native dogs were bred with the small European dogs that ship captains kept on board their vessels to kill vermin, as well as to provide entertainment.

- **1500s**: Increased colonization occurs in New Spain and, as a result, dogs are brought to the New World by colonists from all parts of Europe. In Cuba, these dogs are bred to both native dogs and to the small white dogs that ship captains brought from the Island of Tenerife. These interbred, small, fluffy dogs from Cuba are brought back to Europe for sale. The little white dogs are so enchanting and endearing that they are quickly embraced by Europeans. Thus, although no firm breed identity had yet been established, aggressive breeding caused the numbers of these dogs to expand exponentially both in Cuba and Europe.

- **1700s**: Bichon Havanese is developed in the mid-1700s through careful cross-breeding of toy Poodles, Italian Teneriffes (now the Bichon Frise), and Blanquitos de la Habana.

- **1800s**: By the 1800s, Havanese are so trendy that some become royal dogs and the pets of prominent people, such as author Charles Dickens.

- **1863**: Havanese appear at the Paris Dog Show, listed as Class XXIX "Pet Poodles." This represents the emergence of the Bichon Havanese as an identifiable breed in its own right.

- **1960s**: The Cuban revolution begins, and many of the aristocratic elite flee the country, some taking their little white dogs with them and others being forced to leave them behind. Among the former were the Fantasio, Perez, and Barba families, who manage to leave Cuba with their Havanese.

- **1974**: Dorothy Goodale, a breeder and exhibitor of Afghan Hounds and Irish Setters, hears rumors of the charming little white dogs that escaped Cuba. She and her husband, Burt, collect 11 Havanese dogs from three different breed lines for their kennel. The Goodales then acquire the Barba's six dogs, bringing the total number of Havanese to seventeen in the United States.

- **1979:** The Havanese Club of America (HCA) forms and establishes a registry, which begins the path to breed recognition by the American Kennel Club (AKC), when it recognizes the HCA as the parent club for Havanese in the United States.

- **1983:** The first Havanese is shown in an exhibition in Holland.

- **1988:** Cuba begins the process of repatriating the breed to its home country, with the birth of Cuba Ch. Puppy on December 14.

- **1991:** The Club Cubano del Bichon Habanero is created in Cuba on September 24, advancing the breed there under its guidance.

- **1991:** Havanese are recognized as a breed by the United Kennel Club (UKC).

- **1992:** The Federación Cinológica de Cuba (FCC) works with the Communications Department of Cuba and Cuba's Postal Service to create a series of dog stamps using Cuba Ch. Puppy as the model for a Havanese postage stamp.

- **1993:** Cuba holds its first international dog show, which includes the Bichon Havanese as the only native dog of Cuba.

- **1993:** On October 17, Ch. Puppy, at age 5, enters his first dog show. He competes against five of his offspring and becomes the first Cuban dog to win a Cuban Championship.

- **1996:** The AKC moves the Havanese out of the Miscellaneous class and into the Toy Group class, officially recognizing it as a registered breed.

- **2000:** Ch. Puppy dies on February 15, leaving an impressive progeny to carry on his legacy.

- **2001:** The Havanese standard is AKC approved.

- **2003:** The Havanese Fanciers of Canada are granted accreditation by the Canadian Kennel Club as the official National Breed Club for the Havanese in Canada.

- **2010:** Havanese rise in the AKC rankings from 86th to 31st since being recognized by the AKC in 1996.

Chapter 2

Characteristics of Your Havanese

Ask anyone what makes Havanese special, and you are likely to hear any number of wonderful qualities. They are unique and mischievous. They have a great temperament, and they are affectionate and good with children. They are easy to train. They are sturdy, not frail. Their coat is like silk, and it doesn't shed. And they do the rumba when they walk away from you! While many dog breeds have some of these traits, few possess all of them.

Physical Characteristics

A member of the American Kennel Club (AKC)'s Toy Group, the Havanese is a small but sturdy dog whose body is slightly longer than tall, and whose body outline is more closely rectangular than square. When bred according to the AKC standard, the Havanese will not be mistaken for any other drop-coated dog. Moreover, his coat, which should remain untrimmed, is distinctive in its silkiness and undulates in waves as he walks. His springy, flashy gait is distinctive from other toy breeds. Havanese jump, dance, and twirl, and they are also known for their wild, blitzing behavior, when, for no apparent reason at all, they will take off suddenly, running the perimeter of the yard in acrobatic leaps and bounds. In both structure and gait, the Havanese's form fits his function. Never overly

The Havanese is a small but sturdy dog whose body is slightly longer than tall and whose body outline is more closely rectangular than square.

large or coarse, this agile and energetic little dog is not so fragile that he cannot be a good family pet, and his playful character makes him a charming companion, always ready to entertain you with his athletic antics or to join you in an impromptu romp.

Size

While the official standard for the Havanese breed permits heights from 8.5 to 11.5 inches (22 to 29 cm) at the withers (shoulders), you will find them ranging from 6 to 13 inches (15 to 33 cm). As for their weight, it can range from 3 to 20 lbs (1.5 to 9 kg) or more—which is rather big in a lap dog! When all is said and done, however, a Havanese remains convinced he is a big dog in a small dog's body.

Havanese have almond-shaped eyes and floppy ears.

Body

A Havanese situated more at the medium- to larger-sized end of the breed's size spectrum will, typically, have denser bone. However, his build should not be so dense that he appears coarse; excessive bone is against type. The neck is of moderate length, carried with a slight arch, and blends smoothly into the shoulders. The ribs are well-sprung; the chest is deep and broad in front, and reaches the elbows, which are neatly tucked against the body. The front legs are shorter than the rear legs. This causes the topline to rise slightly as it approaches the rump. Overall, the body presents a rectangular outline rather than a square one.

Head

The head is broad, with ears of medium length attached high on the skull. The muzzle is moderate and should not be flat or needle-pointed. A broad somewhat square nose is desired. The nose should have pigment that is either black or color-appropriate with no pink evident. A scissors bite is preferred. Although a bite that is a bit off will not inhibit the Havanese's ability to make an excellent

COAT CHANGES FROM PUPPYHOOD TO ADULTHOOD

A unique aspect of the Havanese breed is the fact that the dog's coat color changes from birth to adulthood. So, the coat color your puppy begins with is not likely the one he will end up with.

There seems to be a common misconception that cutting off a Havanese puppy's coat will impact color development, but this is simply not true. It will not change the true genetic color of the coat, nor slow down or speed up the change—but it may change the color that you see during the transition from puppy to adult coat. Here's why:

When it comes to genetics, Mother Nature is in control. A puppy whose coat is solid colored from root to tip will still be the same color after his coat is cut. However, in those dogs who have a different colored undercoat or those who have tipped coats (such as sables), there would be a noticeable difference in color after the coats are cut. In Havanese puppies, the newly grown coat, which appears close to the skin, may be lighter colored than the rest of the hair at the ends. So, when the coat is cut, more of the undercoat and/or root color will show, thus making the dog appear lighter colored. Clearly, this does not change what color the coat is genetically or how the color will develop; it simply changes the color you see. Some transitions to adult coats may take up to 12 or 15 months.

These coat color transitions from puppyhood to adulthood are fascinating and beautiful, and they are one of the many special aspects of owning a Havanese.

pet, it might interfere with a show career. Similarly, full dentition is preferred, but partial dentition is accepted as long as it does not interfere with the dog's ability to eat.

Eyes
Ideal Havanese eyes are almond-shaped and dark brown. You should feel as if his eyes can detect the depths of your soul when he looks at you. Dark brown or black eyes are preferred, with an exception for a lighter eye in the chocolate Havanese. All eye rim, nose, and lip pigment should be dark, again with the exception being the chocolate dog, who is allowed to have self-colored pigment or chocolate pigment.

Ears
Havanese ears are floppy, with the ear leather being of moderate length. When extended, they will reach halfway to the nose. They are set high on the skull, broad

at the base, and show a distinct fold. When the dog is alert, the ears lift at the base and perk up.

Tail

The Havanese tail is another element of distinction in the breed. It is high set on the rear and is held resembling a crosier. Plumed with long silky hair, it arcs over the back but is not tightly curled. When the dog is in motion, the tail is carried loosely and may fall straight forward or to either side of the body. Again, the shape of the tail does not inhibit the dog's value as a family pet. However, a dog with a tail that is curled like a pigtail, lies flat over the back, or sticks straight up might not do well in the show ring. Also, the tail may not be docked.

Legs

The front legs should be well-boned, sturdy, parallel, and equal. The distance from the foot to elbow and then from the elbow to shoulder should be equidistant. The upper arm is somewhat short, but the angle between shoulder and upper arm should be sufficient to produce a pronounced fore chest. The elbows turn neither in nor out. The pasterns are short, strong, and flexible, sloping very slightly. The feet are round, with well-arched toes. The dewclaws may be removed.

The hind legs are well-boned, muscular, short, and should be parallel to each other.

The hocks are short and turn neither in or out. Hind feet have well-arched toes and turn neither in nor out. The pads and nails may be black, white, pink, or a combination of these colors. Chocolate dogs may have brown pads and nails.

The dog's "rear assembly" produces a springy gait that is unique to the breed and will sometimes produce the flash of pad that is distinctive to the breed.

Coat

The Havanese was once referred to as the Havanese Silk Dog because his coat is light, airy, and floats or undulates as the dog walks, much like a piece of fine silk. Considered a double-coated, drop-coated breed, both the inner and outer coat are soft to the touch, unlike in other breeds in which the outer coat may be coarse.

The Havanese coat can range from very curly to straight, but a wavy coat is preferred. An ideal coat should be long and untrimmed, but not so long and profuse that it obscures the natural lines of the body. A Havanese in full show coat is a thing of beauty.

In the 1980s, some German breeders began producing litters of Havanese whose coats looked quite different from the specifications in the breed standard. These breedings produced puppies whose coats remained short and smooth into adulthood, with feathered furnishings on the tail, legs, ears, and chest. (This occurs

COAT COLOR LINKS TO HEALTH

Q: I've heard that coat color can affect the health of Havanese. Is this true, and if so, how would it affect overall health?

A: This is a controversial belief, but it may have some basis in fact. As in humans, genes control all aspects of a dog's makeup, from structure to coat color. Genes combine in different ways; sometimes what happens to one gene may affect what happens to another. When a particular condition or disorder repeatedly appears in combination with a specific color or pattern, it is said to be color-linked. Some color-linked conditions have been identified in canines, especially in certain breeds or color types. For example, white-linked deafness is a form of hearing loss linked to the amount of white in the coat, in particular, extensive white on the ears. Color dilution alopecia (hair loss from the body or head) is an abnormality that sometimes occurs in dogs with dilute color coats. In certain instances, a particular type of marbled coat color (called merle) can coincide with deafness and/or blindness.

This does not mean that all dogs with extensive white in their coats, or with color dilution or merle coloration, will develop hair, vision, or hearing problems. However, dogs with these colors or patterns may be more susceptible to carrying or passing along genes that cause these problems. But, the coat color is only one aspect of this situation—the dog also must carry the gene for the disorder.

Havanese come in many colors and patterns, including extensive white and dilute colors, and some also say merle. It's theoretically possible that some version of these disorders may exist in Havanese. Loose associations have been identified in disease cases. However, scientifically proven evidence linking particular disorders to specific coat colors or patterns in the Havanese has not been conclusively established.

—Suzanne McKay began her *Colours of the Rainbow* website, www.havanesecolors.com, some years ago, creating a pantheon of galleries showing the many and varied colors of the Havanese. For an in-depth explanation on the role of genetics in Havanese coat colors, the website offers an extensive scientific discussion on this topic, and much more.

occasionally when two Havanese carrying the gene for a short-haired coat are mated.) Sometimes called a "Shavanese," this is not a recognized variety of the Havanese breed, and although these dogs are as healthy as the long-coated variety, they cannot be shown in the show ring and are not approved for breeding. Additionally, they shed more than one would expect coming from a long-coated or drop-coated breed.

Colors

My assumption is that few people would select a puppy based solely on the color of his coat. But it is difficult to talk about Havanese without taking into account the coat colors that contribute to the uniqueness of the breed.

As noted in the discussion of the breed's history, Havanese originated as white dogs. Currently, it is really quite difficult to find a pure white Havanese who does not have some cream or other dilute (faded) color in his coat. The breed standard for the Havanese permits all colors, singly or in combination, with no preference for one color over another.

One of the best explanations of Havanese colors and markings is provided by Suzanne McKay from Mimosa Havanese kennel in her book, *Colours of the Rainbow*. As she explains, many genes are responsible for coat color in the Havanese. Some genes determine the color itself,

and others affect how the color develops, softens, or fades over time (similar to how bleach can affect colored clothing). Many sable Havanese carry some of these color fading genes. A sable coat for the most part is tipped; this means that the main hair shaft is one color (usually a light color like cream or pale gold) and only the tip of the hair is dark. The proportion of light to dark may be fairly even in a young puppy's coat. However, the length of the tipping does not

Havanese were once referred to as the "Havanese Silk Dog" because their coat is light, airy, and undulates as the dog moves, much like a piece of fine silk.

grow along with the hair. In an older puppy or adult dog with a long coat, most of the hair will be light colored and only an inch (2.5 cm) or so may show dark tipping. As a Havanese puppy matures and the coat grows (or if the tipping is broken or cut off), there will be proportionately less and less dark coat and more light-colored coat. This is why sable dogs seem to get lighter as they mature and why they can look so different from when they were puppies.

Dilute Colors

Dilution, most simply, is a watered down version of a color. An easy way to understand dilution is by making an analogy to a crayon box. If you color with only a black crayon, you will always get black, although you may have softer or more intense shades depending on how heavily you color. If you use both black and white crayons together as you color, you will be diluting the black to shades of gray. In the world of dogs, the dilution of black is called "blue." This is not sky blue or sapphire blue, but rather a soft grayish color with bluish highlights. Dilution not only influences coat color, it also has an impact on tissue pigment (nose, eye rims, lips, and paw pads), as well as on eye color. The tissue pigment can be soft gray/charcoal (rather than black), and the eyes may be hazel, gray, or blue (rather than dark brown).

THE MANY-COLORED COATS OF THE HAVANESE

The following is a list of Havanese coat colors approved by the American Kennel Club (AKC):

- black
- black & silver
- black & silver brindle
- black & tan brindle
- black brindle
- blue
- chocolate
- chocolate brindle
- chocolate sable
- cream
- fawn sable
- gold
- gold brindle
- gold sable
- red
- red brindle
- silver
- silver brindle
- silver sable
- white

Chocolate is an altogether different color; it is not dilute black, although that is a widely held misconception. In the example above, as you dilute a black crayon with white, you will get progressively lighter gray but you will never get brown. Black and brown are two different colors. A chocolate dog is the canine version of a brown crayon. Brown can be pure, or it can be diluted to a pale coffee color. The pigment can be shades of rosy brown or beige, and the eyes may be light brown, hazel, or amber.

Patterns and Markings

As discussed, the coat may be one solid color or have markings in one or more other colors. For example, a multi-colored coat may be sable, black-and-tan, or brindle. Or, it can be pied or parti-colored. Parti-colored markings mean that the color shows in irregular spots. Pied markings follow a distinct pattern, in which the topline is one color, the underline must be white, and the mantle is a solid color covering the shoulders, back, and sides. Pieds must be at least 50 percent white, while partis are at least 50 percent colored.

The most common form of coat patterning is brindle, which is also seen in breeds such as the Boxer and Great Dane. In brindle patterning, there exists sharp patterning between a lighter color overlaid by stripes of darker color. You can see this same patterning in sable Havanese puppies, with the lighter color being cream or gold and the darker color ranging from chocolate to blue, silver, and red.

Choosing and Living With Your Havanese

I come from a ranching and farming tradition in which toy dog breeds were not common. The pets we had doubled as companion and herding or working dogs who occupied a central role in a working farm or ranch. Their jobs were as guardians of livestock and watchdogs, but not too often as cuddly companion dogs, such as the Havanese. It was much later in life that I discovered the Havanese, when I was not even thinking of a toy breed. Like many others, I fell in love with the breed immediately and cannot imagine my home without my Havanese.

Personality

Havanese maintain a whole-hearted devotion to their owners. There's nothing that makes them happier than being the center of attention—your attention—and they will want to be by your side every minute. These intelligent and alert little dogs have extraordinary emotional intuitiveness, often sniffing out a troubled household member before others know there is a problem. Their sensitivity, however, is not without a sense of humor. Havanese are open to being playful but will also become concerned when things go awry. They have very strong social needs, and this should be keenly considered when choosing them as a pet. They love and need their people, enjoy other animals—whether of the dog or cat variety—and adore "little humans" or children.

I once heard a story of a woman who returned her Havanese to the breeder she obtained him from saying, "This dog just follows me around all day. When I'm cooking, he just sits and watches me, then dances for a bite of food." One has to wonder how well she had done her research on the breed.

Sociability

When deciding whether to introduce a Havanese into your family, make sure you understand his breed characteristics thoroughly. Havanese are friendly, gentle, and affectionate dogs who thrive on human companionship and, therefore, do not do well if left alone often. Havanese who do not have adequate company throughout the day may develop separation anxiety or other behavioral problems. For example, it would be difficult for a young, newly married couple who work long hours to properly care for a puppy's needs. Planning for dog sitters, dog walkers, or doggy day care is necessary if your Havanese must be left for long periods of time. Havanese

are generally open to strangers, although there may be an initial timidity upon first meeting someone. But as they get to know you, this timidity will begin to diminish.

Companionability With Other Pets

If you own other pets, bear in mind that larger dogs can cause harm to a smaller dog. Be sure you understand the nature of each breed you have and consider how they will or won't get along. I've placed puppies with clients who had breeds as large as Belgian Sheepdogs, but these dogs were well socialized to other smaller dogs in the household, so the introduction of a Havanese was not a problem. I've had other clients who wanted to introduce a larger dog to their Havanese, and I recommended that they get a very pet-friendly and tolerant breed, such as a Labrador Retriever. Always err on the side of caution and carefully supervise introductions; then continue to supervise all interactions until you are sure that the pets get along well together before leaving them alone. If the relationship won't work, consider rehoming one pet.

Havanese and cats seem to reach a rapprochement pretty quickly, even larger cats such as Rag Dolls, Maine Coons, and some exotic breeds. Early in their ancestry, the breed was kept as a herder of the family's poultry flock, so Havanese should probably not live with a family keeps has birds, especially if the birds are

HAVANESE AND CHILDREN

Before deciding on a Havanese based on reports that he can be silly and entertaining, and thus good with children, you should consider several other factors. First, what are your expectations of a Havanese who is good with children? To a large degree, Havanese enjoy the company of their humans, but they won't enjoy a toddler chasing them, falling on them, or biting their tail. On the flip side, puppies like to nip and chase almost anything with a heartbeat, so supervision will always be necessary whenever your dog and children are together.

I try to place my puppies with families whose children are at least 8 to10 years old. Like many other considerations, this one is not carved in stone, but I take a lot of time to learn about the people who would like to give my dogs a home. Is this a first dog for the adults in the family? If not, what kind of dog did they grow up with? If the parents have experience raising dogs, chances are good that they will be relaxed enough to manage a new puppy around their children. Do they have a game plan if the puppy decides to hang out with one of the children and not the others? It is not uncommon for a Havanese to get along well with everyone in the family but to pick one member to be close to. In one family with whom I placed a dog, the Havanese made friends with one child and stayed close to him for a period of time, and then he would move on to the next child (they had five children!).

Their mild temperament and funny outlook on life make the Havanese a joy to own, but they, like any other dogs, need to be supervised whenever with young children. To make sure your new Havanese adapts well to life in your household, have a trainer come in to teach you how to train basic obedience commands or attend puppy kindergarten classes so that everyone is consistent in maintaining the house rules. This will ensure that both your puppy and your family can live happily together.

accustomed to being outside their cages during the day. I would also not place a Havanese with a family that keeps snakes. Snakes can escape their enclosures and tempt a dog to inspect them. If a Havanese rushes it, sensing he might be a danger, he may well lose the fight if the snake is large or venomous.

Environment

The environment in which your dog lives is important to his physical and emotional well-being. Havanese are very adaptable and do equally well in environments as diverse as an apartment in Manhattan to a farm in Wisconsin, provided that their humans are there with them and their daily care is well thought out and managed.

If you live in an urban area, will the space you live in be large enough for both you and your dog? There is no recommended number of square footage allotted for a Havanese, but remember that the breed is fairly active and will need some space to exercise and play while indoors. Do you have a balcony? Although that can be interesting and fun for your inquisitive Havanese, you must be sure that it is secure because Havanese can and

will climb. Is there a safe and clean doggy park nearby? Your Havanese will need daily walks.

If a suburban environment is in your future, will you have a safe and secure yard? Or a doggy park nearby? How much traffic will there be in your area? The safety of your Havanese is, of course, essential in all environments. Will you live in the country? While traffic might not be as much of a problem in a rural environment, you and your Havanese will face different kinds of obstacles there. You will still need to be vigilant about his safety. Your dog may be to exposed farm equipment or to wild animals roaming

All dogs—even small ones—require sufficient daily exercise every day to remain healthy and happy.

CHARACTERISTICS CHECKLIST

✓ H: Happy, affectionate, and very charming
✓ A: Alerts his people, but is not a continuous yapper
✓ V: Vivacious and trainable—and willing to dance freestyle for food
✓ A: Audacious and almost fearless to a fault
✓ N: Nosy and inquisitive
✓ E: Exuberant, energetic, and entertaining
✓ S: Silky, light coat
✓ E: Easy to live with, bringing lots love and laughter into your life

your property, or he may escape into undeveloped areas and end up lost. Your little dog will need constant supervision while spending time outdoors or away from home.

Exercise

All dogs—even small ones—require sufficient daily exercise every day to remain healthy and happy. Before getting a Havanese, consider the commitment and requirements this will entail. While Havanese will adjust their exercise requirements to their household, they do need regular exercise outside the home. A brisk, short walk or vigorous game in the house or yard will usually be sufficient. They especially enjoy going to dog parks where they can play fetch and run with their pals. Working with your dog in obedience or agility is another great way to get in exercise for both your dog and you—and it's lots of fun.

Trainability

Havanese are intelligent, even-tempered, and unique in their desire to please, so positive training methods are almost always successful. Sensitive to their relationships with their people, though, they can exhibit extreme disappointment and hurt if their human turns her back and ignores them. However, although Havanese like to learn things and are responsive and obedient, they also require training to make sure they don't get too spoiled and bossy. The occasional male may display stubbornness when going through his adolescent phase, but persistence by the trainer can usually push past that. Repetition and consistency are key factors in training. What your Havanese wants and needs is to be loved by his family. As for the rest, there will be missteps and adjustments will have to made. But there is little that cannot be made right with a kiss and big furry hug.

Chapter
3

Supplies for
Your Havanese

You'll need some basic essentials for your Havanese puppy during his first few weeks with you, the first being a crate in which to bring him home safely. Once home, it is best to have everything set up and ready so that his transition into an unfamiliar place is a pleasant and stress-free experience.

Basic Supplies

Before picking up your puppy at the breeder's home, make up a small travel kit consisting of a bottle of water, a small water bowl or cup, a couple of potty pads, some wipes, a roll of paper towels, and a towel. You will also need to bring a harness or collar and leash, and, as mentioned, a travel crate.

You can get these items, as well as other supplies you'll need, at your local pet supply store or order them online from various pet retailers. It helps to prepare a list before shopping, and if you've never owned a dog before, get advice on what to buy from your breeder or vet.

Collar and Harness

Toy dogs have unique needs when it comes to collars. Because these dogs are small, they are more prone to having their esophagus damaged if their leash or collar is jerked too hard or unexpectedly. This is one of the reasons why I begin leash training my Havanese puppies using a small harness. Aside from helping get a

pup used to the idea of wearing one, I do not have to worry that the harness may become caught and cause injury because the D-ring leash attachment is located between the shoulder blades, not at the neck.

There is no age limit for keeping your dog in a harness. How long you use one depends on your preference and what your dog seems more comfortable wearing. Certainly, you can use a flat buckle collar, but I'd recommend waiting until your dog is 6 months old. At that age, Havanese are large enough to avoid accidentally shoving their paw under the collar, getting it stuck, and causing a choking hazard. Ask your breeder whether she recommends a collar or harness. If she has no preference, then ask her to let you know what size collar or harness to purchase about a week before you pick up your pup to bring him home.

Sizing in harnesses is extremely variable because they are all made differently by each manufacturer. Start with a small size and leave the tag on it so you can return it if it does not work. Flat buckle collars are sized in inches; start with 8 inches (20 cm) and go as far as 10 inches (25 cm). When sizing flat buckle collars, you should be able to slip your first two fingers between the collar and the dog's neck and be able to move your fingers back and forth without causing your dog more than minor discomfort.

For safety and comfort, harnesses are the best choice for small dogs. They loop around the shoulders and body so there is no pressure on the neck.

Types of Harnesses

Some toy breed owners prefer using a harness, especially if their dog pulls when walking. Instead of attaching a leash to the dog's collar, a harness loops around the shoulders and body and has a leash attachment on the back so no pressure is placed on the neck.

The step-in harness has become increasingly popular. It functions exactly as its name implies and could not be easier to apply and adjust. The standard (or Roman) harness has been used for a long while and is probably more substantial than needed for a Havanese because it's made of thick canvas. However, if you choose to keep your Havanese in a harness, then the durability of the standard harness will be appreciated. Recent design adjustments by manufacturers have made it easier to apply and more comfortable for the dog.

The V-neck harness is becoming increasingly popular. It combines the

GOING THE DISTANCE...OR NOT

Most breeders are often more than happy to answer any questions you may have about your dog's care, which is especially helpful to people who have never raised a dog. They want to know that their dogs are doing well and that their owners are committed to their proper care. I once received a phone call from a new owner of a Havanese puppy from my kennel: "Something's wrong! Maddie won't move and growls at me when I try to get her to go on our daily walk." By this time, Maddie was only 9 months old, but on the small size for a Havanese. I asked if there had been any changes in lifestyle (no); if elimination was regular (yes); and if she had been eating normally (yes). Then she continued: "Maddie loves our daily walks! She covers those 3 miles like she was a big dog." Three miles! Although I knew she had the best intentions for her dog, she had clearly not read the literature I had given her on Havanese health issues, which emphasized the need to limit exercise to allow the puppy's growth plates to finish growing until around 1 year of age. Maddie was struggling to cover all that ground. Medium-sized Havanese can work up to covering a mile of brisk pacing, but given their small structure, the risk of damage to patellas and hips is greater if you take your Havanese on jogging trips that exceed a mile.

benefits of both the buckle collar and a harness. While it acts like a collar, the V shape leaves the dog's throat area free.

Types of Collars

When choosing your Havanese's collar, remind yourself why you are getting a collar and what activities he will be involved in while wearing it so that you select one that will offer safety and security. The flat buckle collar is the most popular choice.

Collars come in a range of styles and materials, ranging from leather to chain (chain collars are *not* appropriate for Havanese).

Flat buckle collars come in a range of fabrics and types, from corduroy to leather. Style can be your guide here; just be certain to size the collar appropriately as your dog matures.

Martingale collars are becoming more popular with Havanese owners because of the gentle control they allow. Martingales are generally used with dogs who are adamant pullers because these collars tighten slightly with pressure, but with limited constriction. A martingale made with a satin throat cover is popular with people who show their Havanese because the satin covers prevent breaking and tearing of the coat.

Prong (or pinch) training collars should never be used on a Havanese—or on any dogs.

Head collars, which look a bit like muzzles, are used in training and are designed to prevent the dog from pulling on the leash. The only time you might use one is if your dog continues to pull or dart away from you, and you must advance his training to this level.

Leashes

Like collars, leashes come in a variety of colors and styles and can vary in length. Again, bear in mind your dog's size and your own size. I am quite short, so a 6 ft (1.8 m) leash is difficult to manage, although I could use one in a pinch. I recommend a 4 foot (1 m) leash for walking your Havanese. Experiment a little to find what is comfortable for you and your dog.

Standard

Standard, or everyday, leashes are used primarily for basic training and walking your dog. The best material at this stage is a leash made of nylon that is rolled or braided. You can try a braided leather leash on a puppy, but because you will probably be replacing the leash after your puppy has gotten out of the chewing stage, a basic durable nylon or inexpensive leather leash is a better investment.

Adjustable

Adjustable leashes are similar to standard leashes but, as the name implies, they have loops along their length that allow you to shorten or lengthen them as needed. You will find that most of these leashes are made of leather.

Retractable

Operating on the principle of a measuring tape, the retractable leash consists of a retractable cord that rolls back into a plastic case handle. This type of leash offers the freedom of letting your dog wander a bit while on leash. Some argue that it offers a faster response time if your puppy finds himself in danger. However, I encourage new puppy owners not to use a retractable leash until the dog has learned basic commands. Knowing basic commands will reduce pulling and straining at the leash—and, more importantly, ensure your dog's safety.

Crate

When choosing a crate, your dog's size will ultimately help you decide which type to buy. You will also need to consider its uses. For example, if your dog will travel with you, your crate will need to meet the standards of the International Air Transport Association (IATA). Most travel crates are made of hard plastic. You can determine if a plastic crate meets IATA requirements by searching for a certification tag on it. Also, check with any airline you use about its specific measurement requirements. If you need a crate just for local travel or one for the home, you have additional options.

Plastic

Plastic kennels are sturdy, and some are foldable, which is convenient for storage and for travel. They are easy to keep clean; and in some models, the top can be removed and the bottom made into a bed for the dog. They do not, however, grow with the dog, so you'll need to know how to properly size a crate before buying it. Lack of visibility and less air circulation are also drawbacks to plastic crates.

A dog must be able to stand comfortably inside his crate without drawing in his shoulders. He must also be able to turn around easily and stretch out the length of the crate without appearing cramped.

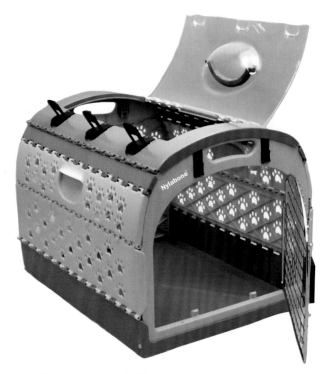

A crate is indispensable when first bringing your puppy home. It provides a safe place for him to stay when you cannot supervise him.

To accommodate the problem of a growing dog and the bother of having to buy another kennel, some manufacturers include a panel that can be placed inside the crate to block off the rear portion; this panel can be moved as he grows.

Wire

Wire crates also come in a wide variety of types and sizes. The sizing recommendations used for plastic crates also apply to wire crate. Some wire crate models also include an adjustable inside panel that allows you to purchase just one crate for the lifetime of your dog.

Wire crates are wide open to view and air circulation; a variety of kennel covers are available to approximate the same level of seclusion as a plastic crate. These crates have the disadvantage of being heavy, and most require assembly. Dogs can sometimes snag nails as well as mouths on the wire. I recommend that dog owners keep a wire crate for house use and a plastic crate for traveling.

Food and Water Bowls

Food and water bowls come in stainless steel, ceramic, and plastic. Most are made to sit flat on the ground, but some are mounted on an elevated platform. Shallow bowls are designed for use by puppies, but puppies can also eat and drink from deeper bowls.

A primary advantage of the steel and ceramic bowls is that they can be put in the dishwasher, and you can be assured they are disinfected and clean. That is not always the case with plastic bowls. And, although offered in many attractive styles and designs, plastic bowls invite the kind of chewing that a puppy seems obsessed with. Additionally, if you plan to show your puppy, be aware that plastic bowls can remove the pigment from his nose as he rubs it against the bowl's side.

Bed

Before selecting a doggy bed, consider how it will be used. For example, is it going to be used outdoors on a deck or patio? Companion dogs, such as the Havanese, are pretty much house dogs, but during nice weather they enjoy sunning on a deck or patio. If the bed is

Stainless steel bowls are best because they are sturdy, easy to clean, and virtually indestructible.

used outdoors, it will need a protective covering or, at the least, it should be machine washable. Second, identify where the bed will be placed in the house. Will it be kept in the kitchen, or on the floor by your bed?

One advantage of having a toy dog such as the Havanese is that his bed doesn't need to be very large. My dogs are born in donut and bumper beds, so I keep several scattered around the house. Every two days, I wash and dry a couple of the beds in rotation; it keeps them clean and fresh, and the soap and hot water kills off any little travelers that may have come home with us after my dogs' last outing.

Grooming Supplies

Even if your dog is taken to the groomer every 6 to 8 weeks to keep his puppy cut the length you want, you will still need to groom your Havanese at home to keep his

DOGGY BED OPTIONS FOR TOY BREEDS

Standard pillow-type dog beds come in all colors and sizes, and are usually square or rectangular in shape. Made like big cushions, they do not have edges or rims. Filling materials are usually made from cotton or polyester. Some people buy cedar chips to stuff inside the bed to control odor. However, if you choose to do this, be sure that the cedar chips are safe for dogs; some are not. An outer and inner cover make maintenance and use of the bed more flexible. If the outer cover is waterproof, it can be removed before washing.

Here are a few types of beds you may consider for a Havanese:

- Nest dog beds resemble standard dog beds, but they have raised side rims, creating a comfortable and cozy place to curl into and snuggle.
- Donut dog beds are typically round, with plush, soft pillow bolsters encircling the bed.
- Orthopedic dog beds are made of foam and are specially designed to provide support and comfort for the dog with joint problems. These often come with covers.
- Kennel dog beds, sometimes referred to as crate pads or bumper pads, are sized to fit inside a crate, but they are often used simply as a pad bed.
- Raised dog beds come in a variety of styles, from simple pipe-framed beds with canvas stretched across, to truly elaborate beds that can only be called doggy furniture. These are made from myriad materials.

long, silky coat healthy and tangle-free. You will need grooming tools, shampoos and conditioners, a grooming table of some sort (you can either buy one produced commercially or build your own), and a hairdryer for drying his coat after bathing.

Brushes and Combs

Brushing and combing your Havanese's coat regularly keeps it healthy and looking good. Brushing helps remove debris and mats, and it helps to distribute the natural oils that keep the coat shiny. I recommend two brushes: a slicker brush and a pin brush. A slicker brush is made of fine wire pins that are bent toward the end of the brush. It is used to remove hair mats. A pin brush has polished or coated pins that don't irritate the skin. It is used for daily brushing or weekly grooming. Brushes with balls on the end of their bristles tend to break the coat and are uncomfortable for the dog.

Before brushing, comb the coat with a standard metal comb, sometimes referred to as a Greyhound comb. In addition to being used to prevent and remove tangles and mats, frequent combing improves the condition of the coat. Metal combs vary in length and teeth spacing. On a Havanese, most people use a 7-inch (18 cm) medium/coarse comb.

Shampoo and Conditioner

When deciding on a doggy shampoo and conditioner, look for ones that are gentle and appropriate for your dog's coat type. While your Havanese is still a puppy, you won't need to use all that much shampoo, and you might consider diluting it. At about 6 months old, add a conditioner because this is when his full coat is beginning to come in and mats begin to form.

Ear and Eye Cleansers

While you have your dog in the bath, it is a good time to clean his ears, using a high-quality ear cleanser and cotton pads to wipe the ear clean.

Many Havanese have a problem with tear staining, particularly when a puppy is cutting teeth and getting vaccinations, but also as adults. Use either a warm washcloth to wipe the eyes clean each morning, or purchase one of the high-quality eye wipes and tear staining treatments available.

X-Pens and Baby Gates

There are times when you will want your Havanese to be safely contained while you may not be able to supervise him. Exercise pens, or x-pens, offer a great alternative to using a crate because they allow your dog a larger area in which to play and exercise. These metal pens fold up for storage and come in a variety of sizes. I've found the 24-inch (61-cm) to 32- or 36-inch (81–91 cm) size is best

SUPPLIES CHECKLIST

Having your pet supplies and home ready for your Havanese's arrival will make his transition to an unfamiliar environment much smoother and more comfortable for him. You'll need:

✓ food and water bowls (2 sets)
✓ food (whatever food your dog is currently eating)
✓ crate and bedding
✓ properly fitted collar, which includes identification tags, and leash
✓ baby gate
✓ canine toothbrush and toothpaste
✓ grooming tools (brushes, combs, etc.)
✓ canine shampoo and conditioner
✓ ear cleaner or (distilled white vinegar mixed with water)
✓ bath mat (nonslip)
✓ towels; coarser towels absorb more water than soft, velvety-type towels
✓ cotton pads and swabs
✓ nail clippers

to accommodate a growing pup. The advantage of being able to slide an x-pen under suitcases when traveling and set them up to keep your dog out of grandmother's garden or off her bed is also a plus.

Many x-pens come with optional tops for added security, and some are made out of decorative white plastic latticework.

Baby gates, which can section off a small area in your home work in much the same way as x-pens, except that they are usually made of wood and mesh (and can and will be chewed on by a puppy). Puppies will be better contained in areas where baby

gates are used, but adult Havanese need something a bit sturdier, such as an x-pen.

Toys

Like other dog products, there is a plethora of toys from which to choose. When selecting toys and chews for your Havanese, safety (which includes appropriate toy and chew size) should always be your first consideration. Some toys are quite flimsy and can be torn into small pieces that can become caught in the dog's throat or cause a blockage in the intestinal tract. It is much safer to choose items that are solid and of dense construction. For example, Nylabone has a wonderful line of toys and edible chews specially designed for puppies and small dogs. Braided ropes with fringe on each end also are excellent toys for puppies and small dogs.

Plush toys are fun, but if the toy contains a squeaker, make sure it cannot be pulled out and swallowed. If the toy has eyes, they should be made of fabric or painted on, not the mechanical kinds used in dolls. It will take a young puppy 2 minutes to chew the eyes off the toy and swallow them, which could be dangerous.

Identification

Your Havanese should be permanently identified for many reasons, but the most important one is recovery if lost. The main means of identification are microchips, tags, and tattoos.

Microchipping

Microchipping involves using a syringe to implant a device the size of a grain of rice under the dog's skin. In the event that your dog gets lost, the chip can be scanned by a rescue volunteer or vet. It will contain, at the least, your contact information so that you can be called and informed of your pet's whereabouts. Microchips can be registered to the company your vet uses, as well as to you.

Most vets will include microchipping during one of your dog's first visits.

Tattoos

In recent years, fewer dog owners have had their dogs tattooed, instead opting for microchipping. If traveling abroad, you might ask if a microchip is satisfactory for identification because many European Havanese arrive in the U.S. tattooed, and

Toys provide excellent opportunities for exercise, mental stimulation, and interaction between pets and their owners.

each country's regulations will vary.

Tags
Metal identification tags that easily attach to a collar and harness are inexpensive and available at your local pet store, vet, and online.

First-Aid Kit
Many new dog owners might not think about one of the most important things that should be included in every arsenal of pet supplies: a first-aid kit. Whether you are at home or on the road traveling, a first-aid kit for your dog is essential.

Canine first-aid kits are available commercially but are easily made up by anyone. First, you'll need a sturdy plastic box in which to keep the items. Here's what you will need:

- hydrogen peroxide for cleansing wounds
- saline solution or eye lubricant
- antiseptic cream

Identification tags can easily be attached to any harness or collar.

PUPPY ANTICIPATION

Q: Now that we have found a breeder we like and have begun collecting the recommended supplies, I find myself becoming increasingly impatient while awaiting the puppy's birth. Is there anything else I can do to prepare for his arrival?

A: Congratulations on your new puppy! And it is not uncommon to begin to feel anxious and impatient waiting to bring him home. Use this time to read informative books about your breed, such as Kathryn Braund's *The Joyous Havanese* and Suzanne McKay's *Woof, Wiggles, and Wags*. Join an online forum, such as the Yahoo group *JustHav Puppies*. Check out Debbie Jensen's website. Although Debbie is a breeder of Shih Tzu, she has put together an excellent little video showing the birth of one her dams. Don't forget the Havanese Club of America (HCA) website! It has much good advice and guidance.

—Candace Mogavero, Faireland Havanese; Delaware AKC Judge, Show Exhibitor, Breeder.

- antihistamine, which works best in liquid form (check with your veterinarian for the correct dosage)
- antidiarrheal medicine (as prescribed by your veterinarian)
- three types of bandages: gauze rolls and pads; adhesive or first-aid tape; stretchy roll bandages
- instruments: tweezers, scissors, magnifying glass
- ice pack

Be sure to store a compact thermal blanket or a small regular blanket with your kit. Keep a list of phone numbers for your vet, a 24-hour emergency clinic, and the ASPCA Animal Poison Control Hotline (1-888-426-4435) in the first aid box, as well as a copy of your pet's current medications and medical record. The ASPCA Poison Hotline is available 24 hours a day and is manned by certified veterinarians. You will be charged a nominal fee per call. For severe poisonings, however, go immediately to your local animal hospital.

Chapter
4

Feeding Your
Havanese

In my experience as a breeder and dog show exhibitor, there are few discussions that can become as volatile as ones concerning which food is best for your new puppy or dog. Humans are passionate not only about their own food but also about what their pet eats. I hand off a puppy to his new family with a sample of the dog food he has been eating. Sometime, within two or three days, I'll get a phone call saying the puppy's tummy is upset. My first question is: "What are you feeding him?" Ninety-five percent of the time the answer is XXX brand or YYY brand—any brand but the one I provided.

So, how do you decide which dog food is best for your Havanese? There is no "one-size-fits-all" food. Choosing the right food for your Havanese requires more than the preferences of you and your puppy. The age, activity level, environment, and current physical condition of the dog will determine the type of diet he requires.

Nutrients are the building blocks of a balanced diet and vital to the continued health of your dog. In this chapter, we look at the different kinds of dog foods that are available, as well as how to read and interpret dog food labels. We will also examine noncommercial food options, such as home-cooked and raw diets, feeding schedules, and diet-related health issues such as obesity.

Achieving a Balanced Diet

How knowledgeable are you about the building blocks of good nutrition for your pet? Do you know the difference between commercial dog food and all-natural and holistic dog food? Understanding how to provide your dog with balanced, optimal canine nutrition will best support his growth, development, and longevity.

Protein

Protein and amino acids are two of the most important elements necessary in your Havanese's diet. Amino acids make up the building blocks of protein and enable them to be stored until they're ready to be used. Proteins support structural growth and development, as well as strengthen the immune system.

But how much protein does your dog need? Puppies require more protein than do adult or performance dogs, as do pregnant and nursing females. Generally, your puppy's food should contain 28 percent protein, while adults require 18 percent and performance dogs require 25 to 35 percent. Nursing females require 28 percent. So, clearly, the stage of life and the activity level of your dog is important in assessing proper dietary needs.

Fats

Aside from making food taste better, fats are an important source of concentrated energy. They are needed to transport

The age, activity level, environment, and current physical condition of your dog will determine the type of diet he requires.

and store vitamins. They also contribute to a healthy coat and skin. Fats produce essential fatty acids, such as omega-3, -6, and -9, which extend lifespan, reduce inflammation, and maintain heart health. Because essential fatty acids are difficult for the body to synthesize, they must be obtained through diet.

Carbohydrates
One of the most astonishing findings in canine nutritional studies is that dogs do not need carbohydrates. They will eat them willingly, and in as much quantity as they can, but they are not necessary to their well-being. However, carbohydrates are a convenient source of energy. The pet food industry has used carbohydrates for their convenience, abundance, and long shelf life. Most often made from grains, these foods do not offer substantial nutrition, but they do offer some nutrients that dogs need. Select foods that contain grains such as barley, brown rice, and oatmeal, which

are highly digestible and contain vitamins, minerals, fats, and some protein. It's best to limit refined carbohydrates and opt for more nutrient-rich foods.

Vitamins and Minerals

Micronutrients are made up of vitamins, minerals, and enzymes. Vitamins are organic compounds that perform essential bodily functions. They help the body to absorb nutrients and minerals, regulate metabolism, fight disease, and function and grow normally. Minerals play a role in almost every function in the body as well. They work in conjunction with other minerals, vitamins, and enzymes to aid in the formation of bones and cartilage, the functioning of muscles and nerves, the production of hormones, the oxygenation of blood, and more.

Most high-quality commercial foods provide the amount of nutrients needed. And, in fact, supplementing your dog with vitamins without consulting your veterinarian might lead to nutrient toxicity. If you are wondering if you should add supplements to your Havanese's diet, consult your veterinarian.

Commercial Dog Foods

Havanese do not need specialty food, but they do need quality food. Commercially prepared dog foods come in dry, semi-moist, and canned varieties. All these foods offer convenience; they're easy to prepare and feed, and you can easily track the amounts eaten. But are they equal in quality?

Dry Foods

Dry dog foods are the most popular

Dry foods provide the most popular and diverse meal base for dogs.

READING COMMERCIAL DOG FOOD LABELS

All ingredients in commercial dog foods must be listed on the packaging label in order of weight; the ingredient of greatest quantity in the food appears first on the list. Reading the guaranteed analysis section on the label will tell you what is contained in the food and how much of each ingredient is in it.

When looking for a good choice, the two most important ingredients to check for are proteins and fats. Some type of meat, whether beef, chicken, meat meal, fish, or fish meal, should appear first or second. Fatty acids, which can include fish meal, fish oil, or flaxseed oil, should appear near the top of the list as well. Premium versions of dry dog foods will contain at least 17 to 23 percent protein and 10 to 12 percent fat.

To evaluate a dog food you are considering, you may want to check it against the nutritional chart provided by the Association of American Feed Control Officials (AAFCO) entitled Dog Food Nutrient Profiles. Visit the AAFCO website at www.aafco.org.

Also read the label to determine the manufacturer and distributor of the product. As more dog foods and treats are being imported, we have seen an increasing number of pet food recalls and illnesses occurring from products that do not come from countries that regulate their foods as rigorously as does the United States.

meal base for dogs. Aside from convenience, they are usually the most affordable option. However, commercial kibbles often have higher levels of grains in the ingredient list, making them more difficult to digest. Also, nutrients are lost in the manufacturing process and must be added back in, sometimes in less accessible forms. If your dog likes to nibble throughout the day, dry food can be safely left out in bowl for him. Another advantage of dry kibble is that its crunchiness aids in controlling tartar on teeth.

Semi-Moist and Canned Foods

Semi-moist and canned food are pricier, but dogs often like them because they are tasty and have stronger aromas. Quite often they contain less grains and more fats and protein. Some even have less or no preservatives than dry foods. They also have the advantage of traveling well. However, they contain a lot of water, so

TRANSITIONING YOUR PUPPY TO ANOTHER FOOD

Whenever you change dog foods—whether transitioning to another brand or to an adult food—do so gradually to prevent upsets. Here's a feeding guide you can follow:

- **Day One:** Feed only the food that your puppy has been fed by the breeder. If he does not eat much for a day or two, do not be alarmed.
- **Day Two:** Replace ¼ of the current kibble with the new dog food.
- **Day Three:** Replace ½ of the current kibble with the new dog food.
- **Day Four:** Switch over to the new food completely.

you get less for your money. And wet foods can also affect dental health, so you'll need to brush your dog's teeth more often.

Natural/Holistic Versus Premium Dog Foods: What's the Difference?

With the increasing number of pet food recalls recently, it is little surprise that there has been increased interest in offering organic and natural foods, as well as noncommercial home-cooked and raw foods. However, it can be very confusing when one is looking at the growing list of commercial dog foods claiming to be holistic or natural. Most of these terms are marketing terms because, legally, there is not much difference between these foods and premium foods. And there is no accepted definition of holistic or

natural dog food. Dog foods promoting themselves as natural claim they do not contain any synthetic products. However, some nutrients needed by a dog can only be obtained through synthesis. Baking powder, for example, is a synthesized product used in some dog foods. The Association of American Feed Control Officials (AAFCO), which monitors and certifies pet foods, has declared that if a dog food contains any synthetic ingredients, it must bear a disclaimer label showing the consumer that there are, in fact, such ingredients in the product.

Home-Cooked Diets for Dogs

So why would anyone want to cook for their dogs? Sarah Abood, DVM, Ph.D., and assistant professor of small animal clinical sciences at the Michigan State

University College of Veterinary Medicine, has observed a steady increase in pet owners cooking for their dogs over the past 10 years. She notes, however, that interest really peaked after the melamine-tainted dog food scare in 2007. Advocates of home-cooked diets are steadfast in the belief that they provide a very healthy alternative to processed commercial foods because the food is fresher, more wholesome, and preservative-free, and because you can control and know what your dog is fed.

Home-cooked diets for dogs come in several variations. One can decide to add no bones or meat to the diet or to add raw bones and/or meat to cooked grains and vegetables. Or, one can choose among several types of dog food mixes. A dog food mix is designed as a base to which you add fresh foods such as meat, eggs, and dairy (yogurt, kefir, cottage cheese) in order to provide a complete diet. These dog food mixes claim to provide a complete diet when fresh foods are added per instructions, but their company websites provide little nutritional information and make no mention of AAFCO values on their websites. They should be fine to use as part of a rotation with regular commercial dog foods, but should not be fed exclusively until certified by AAFCO.

Whether you choose to feed your dog a home-cooked diet or commercial dog food, it should contain the healthiest ingredients possible.

Adding Supplements

An ideal home-cooked dog meal is complete and balanced. But an ideal is only something to aspire to, so the question arises: to supplement or not to supplement?

Special vitamin and mineral mixes are available to use in balancing out incomplete homemade diets, including supplying the proper amount of calcium. Note that these are different from the traditional vitamin and mineral supplements designed to be added to complete diets.

Most home-cooked dog meals will require some kind of supplementation. Because the heat of cooking destroys many nutrients in homemade ingredients, supplements are especially important to ensure optimum nutrition. Fish oil or cod liver oil are excellent supplements, especially for coat maintenance in the Havanese. Vitamin E should be automatically added if you are using fish oil or plant oil.

A continuing and underlying concern is providing adequate levels of calcium, no matter what variety of home-cooked diet you choose. Calcium isn't stored in the body in the same manner as other nutrients. It does its job and leaves the body, thus it needs to be replaced frequently. However, an overabundance of calcium, particularly in puppies and young dogs whose growth plates have not yet closed, can cause problems in the bones. Vitamin and mineral enriched chew treats like the ones manufactured by Nylabone provide dogs with necessary calcium. The advantage of these chews is that they allow the proper amount of calcium to enter the body slowly, over a period of time. They're made with chicken and are simple to feed. Before deciding on what kind of calcium and the dose required, be sure to check with your veterinarian.

If you prefer to feed a home-cooked or raw diet, discuss this option with your vet before doing so.

THE RAW FOOD DIET

Q: How do I properly feed my dog a raw food diet?

A: If you follow these raw food diet feeding tips, you should be off to a good start. However, always consult with your vet before beginning any new feeding or health-related program.

- Buy meats from a trusted source. If possible, purchase organic, free-range chicken and human-quality grass-fed beef. Use only fresh vegetables and fruits.
- After preparing or serving raw food, wash your hands and clean and disinfect all kitchen surfaces to ensure food safety for your dog and your family.
- Freeze prepared portions in amounts suitable for single-day use and defrost daily.
- As you use a daily portion, remove the next day's serving and thaw it in the refrigerator.
- Add a probiotic supplement such as plain yogurt with live cultures to your dog's daily ration to assist digestion.
- Remove uneaten portions after being left out for 30 minutes and refrigerate them for use later in the day, but do not hold them longer than 24 hours.

—Robin Moser, Havana Silk Dogs Havanese; Exhibitor, Breeder, and Author.

Researching Your Meal Plan

It is not too surprising that the American Veterinary Medical Association (AVMA) has been quite slow to support home-cooked meals for dogs. Dr. Roger Mahr, DVM and president of AVMA, strongly discourages feeding table scraps since one cannot accurately evaluate the amount of nutrients provided in them. He notes that the added gravies and fats in table scraps have led to an increased incidence of diabetes in our pets. Dr. Tony Buffington, DVM, warns against alternating commercial foods with home-cooked meals because it is difficult to match the complete nutrition offered by commercial dog foods using such a plan, and equally difficult to monitor your dog's intake of certain nutrients as well.

An excellent example is the need to monitor vitamin D, which is already adequately available in nonsynthetic ingredients in many commercial foods. Adding excess vitamin D to the diet increases the risk of overdoses that can eventually result in the death of the dog.

If you're still determined to feed a home-cooked diet, Buffington recommends that you first sit down and discuss this option with your vet. He also recommends www.petdiets.com, which is considered one of the best websites on home-cooked pet diets.

Raw Food Diets

Formally called either the Biologically Appropriate Raw Food diet or the Bones and Raw Food (BARF) diet, this feeding method remains one of the most controversial issues in veterinary medicine. The primary difference between a raw food diet and a home-cooked diet is that approximately 80 percent of the food is raw and includes meat products such as chicken necks, backs, and wings, or beef bones. The remainder of the diet is composed of fruits and vegetables, eggs, and dairy products, which are also provided raw. (An important note is to never feed cooked bones to dogs.

Cooking causes the bones to become brittle, increasing the likelihood that they will splinter and get caught in the throat or lodged in the intestines.)

Supporters of the raw food diet are as passionate as those in opposition to it. Among the claims made by advocates of the raw diet is that it makes the coat more shiny and healthier looking, that it dramatically strengthens the immune system, and that teeth stay cleaner and healthier, with fewer incidents of gum disease. The problem with claims both for and against feeding a raw diet is that no persuasive scientific evidence is available to either side. Some issues that make a raw diet less attractive are the amount of time it takes to prepare, safety issues involved in handling raw ingredients, and balanced supplementation. In an effort to find a middle ground between the true home-prepared raw diet and other dog foods, a commercial alternative has been developed and is available at

Limit the number of treats you offer your dog to keep him trim, and make sure they consist only of healthy ingredients.

FEEDING SCHEDULE

Once you get your Havanese, be sure to ask the breeder ahead of time what kind of food he has been eating and how much and at what times he has been fed. Typically, if he is about 10 to 12 weeks of age, he is still eating three meals a day, plus receiving one or two treats. Treats are usually used in conjunction with training, so it is wise for these to be offered separately.

Feeding schedules must be determined by your or your family's daily routine, but the following is typically the schedule I use for my dogs:

- **6:30 a.m.: Breakfast.** If you do not plan on free feeding (allowing dog food to remain accessible throughout the day), then leave the bowl down only 20 to 30 minutes and pick it up and refrigerate any leftovers. Of course, if you choose to free feed, leave out kibble or other food that does not need refrigeration. Some households need to free feed because of their lifestyle, but it also means that there might well be poop to pick up when they get home. Your puppy will let you know when he is moving away from three feedings a day by eating less (leaving more food in the dish).
- **12:00 p.m.: Potty break.** After getting some exercise, reward your dog with a treat. If your puppy is less than 4 months old, provide a noon meal, followed by exercise and a potty break.
- **Mid-Afternoon: Potty break.** After getting some exercise, reward your dog with a treat.
- **6:30 p.m.: Dinner.** Repeat the same routine as breakfast, except that you should discard any remaining food left in the bowl.

I strongly recommend that you do not switch dog foods until your new dog has had a chance to settle in; changing foods too quickly can cause uncomfortable digestive upsets. It is also preferable not to change dog foods too often since it will send the message that if your dog waits long enough he will get fed an even better food.

many pet stores. Complete with feeding instructions, these freeze-dried raw food meals are safe, offer long-term storage, and are easy to feed.

Treats

The best treats for your Havanese are healthy ones fed in moderation. Always offer treats that are low in fat, salt, and sugar, and preservative free. A good commercial choice is something like Nylabone chew treats or bones, which include vitamins, minerals, and omega-3s. Marrow bones are strictly recreational and have no nutritional value. I do feed my Havanese marrow bones, but I am very careful about the size. Bigger is better because there will be less chance of the treat getting lodged in the dog's throat. I do give rawhide but not rolled rawhide, which can also being chewed off into small pieces and become lodged in the throat or cause intestinal blockage. I like the flat flip chips that force a dog to gnaw around the edges. It goes without saying that your dog should always be supervised when be given this type of chew.

Of course, "real food" treats are always a great option; just make sure that any treat you provide is healthy, safe, and appropriate for dogs.

How Much to Feed

When you pick up your new Havanese—whether he is a

A healthy diet combined with daily exercise is needed to ensure and control proper weight.

Check It Out

FEEDING CHECKLIST

✓ Know the building blocks of good nutrition for your pet to ensure he is fed a complete and balanced diet.

✓ Research and weigh the pros and cons of commercial, home-cooked, and raw diets.

✓ If you decide to feed a home-cooked or raw diet, discuss this option with your vet before doing so.

✓ Observe the same safe handling practices for your dog's food as for your own foods.

✓ The best treats for your dog are healthy ones fed in moderation.

✓ With the help of your vet, choose whether to give supplements.

✓ Changing dog foods should be done gradually, whether switching from commercial or noncommercial foods.

✓ The amount fed a toy dog like the Havanese can be as much as 4 to 5 percent of his body weight daily.

✓ A healthy diet combined with daily exercise is needed to ensure and control proper weight.

10-week-old puppy or an adult—ask your breeder what your dog's feeding schedule has been and what and how much he is being fed. Over time, I have found that puppies 10 to 16 weeks of age need to eat 1/3 cup (2.3 oz) of dog food three times a day. Your puppy will let you know when he is ready to cut down on his food. I feed my junior and adult dogs 1/2 cup (4 oz) twice a day. Some advocate once a day feedings, but these are small dogs with small stomachs. Additionally, my Havanese seem calmer if they have two meals a day.

Obesity

Just as obesity is on the rise in humans, it is also on the rise in dogs. A healthy diet combined with daily exercise is needed to ensure and control proper weight. Dog obesity programs recommend a higher level of protein with a moderate amount of high-quality fats and a smaller percentage of carbohydrates, plus a minimum of two walks or exercise sessions a day. And remember that treats count toward calorie intake, so feed them sparingly and offer low-calorie healthy ones.

Chapter
5

Grooming Your
Havanese

F ew things in the world are as awe-inspiring as a freshly groomed Havanese in full show coat. Yet it is not uncommon to hear, "We just want a Havanese as a family pet, not a show dog." Such a statement assumes a difference that only exists in the long term: A family pet will usually end up in a puppy cut and, of course, a Havanese show dog will be wearing his stunning coat through to earning a championship title at the least.

But what does a pet Havanese have in common with a show Havanese? They both begin to receive grooming in the same place: the whelping box. One can talk about early socialization, but what exactly might that mean in terms of grooming? Chances are your pup has received some form of grooming prior to being sent home with you, first from his mother and then from his breeder. Ask your breeder how your new puppy handles being in the bath. I have found that I can bathe my pups in the utility room sink with a sprayer beginning at about 6 weeks of age, and they are fine with it. However, at about the 8-week mark, they begin resisting, and I have to secure them to avoid having them injure themselves. Also, before they reach the 8-week mark, I lay them in my lap and stroke them lightly

Whether you choose to keep your Havanese in a short puppy cut or a show coat, he will need to be brushed regularly.

Check It Out

GROOMING CHECKLIST

To groom your Havanese, you will need the proper tools and supplies:

✓ canine ear wash
✓ canine eye wash
✓ canine shampoo and conditioner
✓ coarse big-toothed comb
✓ cotton pads
✓ cotton swabs
✓ doggy toothbrush and toothpaste
✓ eye and ear wipes for daily use
✓ flea comb
✓ hair dryer (optional)
✓ pin brush (small)
✓ scissors, blunt-nosed
✓ scissors, small, sharp
✓ slicker brush (small)
✓ stainless steel comb
✓ thick towels

with a comb or brush, and I take a cotton swab and move it in and out between the toes, under the nails, and around the dew claws. So, if you pick your pup up between his 10th and 12th week, he should be accustomed to handling and familiar with basic grooming.

Grooming may sound pretty straightforward at first, but it does require some preparation and commitment. It is important to have your puppy well socialized to the bath process so that you both do not resist grooming, which just makes matters worse and often leads to

problems like matted fur that becomes impossible to untangle. I am often asked how often a puppy should be bathed. And, again, there is no straightforward answer beyond: when he is dirty! Show dogs, of course, are groomed more often, but both a family pet and a show dog share the same need for regular brushing. With some dogs, depending upon what stage of growth they are in, you can get by with brushing three to five times a week. It will take about 10 minutes, and it is a pleasant activity that will offer a good bonding experience.

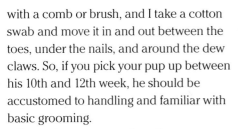

Brushing

Brushing is the first step in the grooming routine, and this is where the difference between care of a family pet kept in a puppy cut and a show dog kept in full show coat comes into play. The show dog will take much longer to brush out than the family pet. Here, I'll only discuss the home grooming of a family pet because most show dogs are taken to professional groomers.

Line brushing or line combing is a thorough and gentle way to get debris and mats out of your pet's coat. While your dog is lying on the table, gently take one hand and push the hair back in the opposite way from which it grows. With your pin brush or comb, gently pull the hair down one small row at a time; this is called line brushing. To remove any mats, first see how much of the mat you can pull apart with your fingers. Then roll the mat over one finger and gently begin separating it with a comb.

Before bathing your dog, comb and brush his coat thoroughly to remove any tangles or mats.

Puppy Love

PUPPY BATH TRAINING

Before you actually bathe your Havanese puppy, it is helpful to acclimate him to bathing by making it as stress-free and enjoyable as possible. By practicing the following bath training techniques, he will gradually learn to trust you and accept bathing as part of his usual grooming routine.

First, place your puppy inside a dry tub (or sink if you will bathe him there) on a nonslip bath mat. Offer him some treats or a toy. Play with him by wiggling the toy in his mouth or ask him to sit and give him a treat—anything that will make the experience of being in the tub pleasant and rewarding. You want your puppy to feel safe and secure there. Praise him lavishly for behaving and being calm. After a few minutes, remove him from the tub. Do this exercise every day for about a week, keeping him there a bit longer until he can remain in the tub for about 10 minutes.

Once your puppy accepts this calmly, move on the next step. Run some warm water into the tub, but only enough to cover his feet. Place your puppy into the tub slowly while speaking softly to him and playing with him to distract him. Let him get used to the water and wet him down if he will allow it. Repeat the rewards and praise as you did before, offer him a treat when you are done, and take him out of the tub. Towel him dry and tell him what a good boy he was. Then offer him another treat. Do this exercise several times, until he is comfortable being in the water.

Once your Havanese is comfortable being in the water, it is time to have an adult doggy bath! Be sure to offer lots of praise and rewards throughout the entire process to keep it a positive experience.

Pay particular attention to your dog's legs, as well between his toes, where knotting is more prone to appear. Also check each armpit for knots because they frequently appear there; in these sensitive areas, I recommend trimming mats out rather than putting your puppy through the trauma of brushing them out. After a thorough brushing and combing, your Havanese is ready for his bath.

Bathing

Before putting your dog in the bath, have your supplies assembled and ready to go. You will need dog shampoo and conditioner, towels, and a hair dryer if you choose to use one.

Safety First

Always ensure that your dog is safe in the tub. Never fill it more than a few inches (cm) deep, and make sure the water is not too hot or too cold. At about 4 months of age, a puppy begins transitioning to the equivalent of an adolescent stage. He has lots of ideas about what he should do, and bathing generally isn't one of them. I strongly urge all puppy owners to be sure to secure their dogs safely in the sink or tub. This can be done by leaving his collar on while bathing and attaching it to his leash, which is shortened and tied around the water faucet. Once your dog learns to accept the process, this may no longer be necessary.

Bathing your dog helps to remove dirt and debris, prevent mats from forming, and makes him smell good.

How to Bathe Your Dog

Before beginning the bath, put cotton in your dog's ears to minimize water getting into the ear canal. You may also put a drop of mineral oil into each eye to keep water from getting into them.

While a puppy is still at my kennel, I use a gentle shampoo only. I am not too concerned about conditioning a puppy's coat at this early stage. As a puppy gets older and his coat changes from a juvenile to a full adult coat, I begin adding conditioner. As an economic measure, fill a plastic bottle half full of shampoo and half full of conditioner and use that on your puppy.

Apply the shampoo/conditioner after you have thoroughly wet your dog down. Using your hands, gently rub it into the coat, beginning at the head and gradually working your way down the torso to the end of the tail. Be sure not to get soap in his eyes or water in his ears. Do not rub the coat back and forth or all the mats you removed will return. Next, work the lather into each of the legs.

After you have finished lathering the coat, rinse it thoroughly, being careful to remove all soapy residue. Hold his beard as you spray water over his head, down his back, and down his legs. Never spray water in your dog's face. Again, be sure you have removed all shampoo/conditioner.

When you've finished rinsing, wrap a towel around your dog and gently pat him dry. Again, do not rub the coat back and forth with the towel. When the towel is wet through, using another dry towel to get the remaining water out of the coat. Run a coarse comb through the coat, using the line brushing technique describer earlier. You may choose to let the coat air dry at this point or use a hair dryer to blow it out.

Ear Care

Floppy-eared dogs such as Havanese require a bit more ear care than other dogs. The dark, warm ear canal, which is deprived of sufficient air circulation by the long ear flap, is a prime place for developing yeast infections and becoming infested with ear mites. So, keeping the ears clean and free of debris and wax is the first order of business if you want to prevent ear infections. There are many excellent ear washes on the market, but check with your vet to see which she prefers. I use an ear wash on my dogs weekly.

How to Clean the Ears

Put the prescribed amount of ear wash into the dog's ear, and rub at the base of the ear to loosen wax and debris. Leave the wash in for 10 minutes. Using a clean cotton pad, remove the dirt and debris. You can squeeze the base of the ear to push up any remaining ear wash in the ear. Repeat these steps until the ear wash is clear and the cleansing pads look clean.

Eye Care

The best eye care is preventive, and this can be accomplished with a once weekly eye wash. When you take your puppy in for his first health check, ask your vet which eye wash she prefers.

How to Groom the Eyes

Hair should be kept out of the eyes, so regularly trim around the eyes, being especially careful to trim around the inner

TO CUT OR NOT TO CUT

Q: I often keep my Havanese in a short puppy cut, but will he need extra protection in the summer and winter months, not having a full coat?

A: A: Havanese have an outer coat that is light and feels like raw silk. They also have a slightly heavier undercoat that insulates the body from the sun, thus making the breed more heat tolerant than some others. But despite the heat tolerance offered by their double coat, they can and will get sunburned in those areas where the coat is thinner or if the coat is kept in a short puppy cut. Havanese enjoy outdoor and beach activities with their humans, so if you often participate in these activities with your dog you may want to apply sunscreen; check with your vet to see what she recommends. Havanese will need protection in the winter when it gets really cold, so you may want to keep the coat longer or provide a doggy jacket when outdoors.

—Natalie Armitage, Overlook Havanese; Exhibitor and Breeder.

corners. Use only blunt-nosed scissors to do this.

Daily wiping of the eyes using specialized eye wipes or simply a warm washcloth can help to keep eyes healthy and staining to a minimum. Also check to see if there is hair in the inner canthus of the eye. Hair acts as a natural wick, and the steady poking can cause irritation as well as excess tearing. Hair brushing into the eyes should be trimmed.

Tear staining is a particular problem for Havanese. Staining occurs when there is an overflow of tears onto the cheeks. The interaction of normal bacteria with tears on the hair and skin causes the hair color to change. How much and how often this occurs depends on your dog's pedigree line, as well as on how acute the tear staining may be. Your puppy might come home with tear staining. It is not unusual for this to become acute while he is getting vaccinations and cutting teeth, but it should clear up by the time he is a year old. (For an in-depth discussion of tear staining, its causes and cures, check out Bhejei Maltese at www.bhejei.com/tearsta.htm.)

Dental Care

During the past decade, there has been a growing awareness of the increase of dental disease in our family pets, and the importance of maintaining good dental hygiene is now understood to be crucial to overall health. Part of the reason for this problem has to do with changing diets, with our dogs not having as many opportunities to eat truly crunchy food. Toy breeds like Havanese are particularly prone to dental disease because the small size of their mouth does not allow for easy cleaning, which is necessary on a regular basis. Another reason for the upsurge in concern over dental issues is that oral hygiene has been one of the most overlooked areas of professional care. By the time one realizes a Havanese puppy has gum disease, the accumulation of plaque and tartar is already well under way.

How can you know if your dog has dental disease? Symptoms can include bad breath, inflamed gums, difficulty or pain when chewing, decreased appetite, and in advanced cases, loss of teeth and loss of weight. Have your dog's teeth examined by your vet at every checkup. Annual dental cleaning under an anesthetic may also be advisable for toy breeds. If your Havanese is still a youngster, this may be a good time to check for and remove any remaining deciduous or baby teeth while the vet is doing this cleaning.

As with many health-related issues, prevention is the best first step. With recommendations from your veterinary dentist, set up a regular regimen for checking the condition of your dog's teeth and gums, as well as for brushing daily with a toothbrush and toothpaste made for dogs. Another way to get ahead of dental disease is to use dental chews such as the ones made by Nylabone, which are specially designed to get into those small crevices to help control tartar and plaque while freshening breath.

Nail Care

Nail care is perhaps one of the more neglected aspects of grooming. Puppies

In addition to brushing, offer your Havanese treats designed to break down tartar and plaque.

GROOMING AS A HEALTH CHECK

Grooming provides an excellent time to perform a routine health check on your Havanese. Here's how:

Eyes: As you comb the hair back from your dog's eyes, inspect them for signs of anything unusual. Is there any redness, either on the eyeball itself or on the eye rims? Is there more eye drainage than normal? Does the eye have an odor, or is there any indication an infection may be present? Healthy eyes should appear clear and bright.

Ears: Smell your dog's ears often. Yeast infections are the curse of the floppy-eared dog, and a foul odor is one of the first indicators. Does the ear seem to be secreting more ear wax than normal? I find that my chocolate or red-colored Havanese seem to secrete more ear wax, which, in turn clumps onto the ear hair, so I keep their ear hair pulled out a bit more than I do on the other dogs. Also inspect for any signs of debris that may indicate parasites such as mites, and check behind the ears to see if there are any cuts or abrasions. Healthy ears will not have an odor or waxy buildup, and they will look clean.

Mouth: Pull your dog's lips back to check the condition of his mouth. Check the teeth and gums to see if they are in good condition, and look for loose, broken, or overgrown teeth or signs of redness or swelling in his gums. Healthy gums are firm and pink, black, or spotted, just like your dog's skin, and healthy teeth are smooth and white. If there is redness or inflammation, bleeding, yellow or brown discoloration on the teeth, foul breath, or drooling, your dog needs veterinary attention right away.

Nails: Nails should be kept at a manageable length. Check the toes for torn toenails, and check the pads for cracks, cuts, or bruises.

Nose: A healthy nose should be wet and cold, and without any discharge.

Body: Check the skin for redness, bumps, breaks, or abrasions, and if you live in a rural area, check for anything that might look like a bite. If you find anything unusual, or there are affected areas that won't heal, take your dog to the vet for treatment.

Reproductive area: This area should be clean, with no drainage of any kind, and should not emit an odor.

Anal area: Some dogs have problems with impacted anal glands, which will be evidenced by excessive licking of the anal area and scooting the bottom across the floor. If you suspect this problem, take your dog to his vet. She can take care of this, as well as show you what needs to be done, if you are willing to take on this grooming chore yourself.

do not like it much, and owners are often afraid they may hurt their puppy during the process. Chances are your Havanese is not running in the woods or working out on concrete several hours a day to keep his nails dull. So they grow and grow, and eventually become so long and curved nails that it is painful for him to walk. Long nails are also vulnerable to being torn off. Keeping your dog's nails trimmed is a necessary part of maintaining basic foot health.

Your Havanese will need to have his nails trimmed about every 4 to 6 weeks. There are two ways to trim nails: one uses standard nail clippers, and the other uses a Dremel tool to grind them down. I alternate between using both tools, depending on the tolerance of the dog to each one. For an anxious, squirmy puppy, I use ergonomic, professional nail clippers. They have ribbed, nonslip handles that provide a safe and secure approach, lessening the risk of injury.

I also use guillotine-type nail clippers, but I find it difficult to use them safely with fidgety puppies. I use the Dremel tool mostly on my show dogs—and that is primarily because they let me! It does put a nicer finish on the clipped nail. Be careful not to let hair get caught in the rotating part of the grinder, which will cause pain and make your dog run whenever he sees this tool come out of your grooming tool kit.

Whether you use clippers or a grinder, you must also be careful not to cut into the quick, which is a highly sensitive area of the nail. If you clip this part of the nail, it will bleed, cause pain, and frighten your dog. Because it is difficult to see the quick, particularly on chocolate, red, or black Havanese whose pigment is self-colored, remove only a small amount of the nail at each trimming session. I strongly recommend that you have your veterinarian show you how to trim nails properly before you do it for the first time.

Chapter
6

Training Your Havanese

While we know that dog ancestry dates back about 15,000 years, it is only speculation as to when dogs formed the bond with humans we see developed today. During the hunting/gathering period, dogs and humans learned to live together, and the seeds of obedience training began. During this time, dogs acted as our protectors against predators and as hunters, bringing us small game they killed for our food. Development of the agricultural or pastoral period offered increased stability for humans and dogs alike. The kinds of dog training that occurred at this time were related to work. For example, working dogs were trained to obey commands as they joined humans in herding livestock. Sporting dogs were companions for hunting and bringing home game. Some cultures incorporated their dogs into task-specific training, such as cartage to pull sleds or food carts to the village. Over time, dogs needed to learn to adapt to their human partners in order to live with them successfully and to be accepted as part of their human pack. All dogs need boundaries and appreciate knowing what is expected of them, and they will work hard to please their owners if they are treated with patience and love.

The Importance of Training

So why train your dog? Learning to live as a "good citizen" is paramount to a dog's safety, as well as to his acceptance into the family household and community. More dogs than I want to think about end up in a shelter because their families didn't know how to train them, didn't have the time to train them, or just thought their dogs would come already trained. It would seem self-evident that a puppy would need training, just as a child needs rearing. Yet, I am quite often asked by clients if the puppy they are interested in taking home is housetrained or obedience trained. Some even ask this of older dogs they are considering. The point I'd like to get across here is that training your dog goes on, at some level, throughout his life. Even if a puppy or adult is potty trained at my house, he will still have to be taught the house rules and what is expected of him when he arrives at his new home to live with another family. Also, more and more cities or towns, as well as landlords, are requiring evidence that a dog has been trained. Training is also necessary if you choose to participate in some sporting activities, competitions, or volunteer work with your dog.

Positive Training

Why is positive training preferable, and what, exactly, does it entail? In 2004, the Universities Federation for Animal Welfare (UFAW) performed a study on pet dogs across a wide spectrum. Also included were working dogs (guide dogs, drug-sniffing dogs, police and military dogs). The study is unique because the dogs were studied in their home and working environments instead of in a laboratory. The authors found that there was a correlation between the type of training used (positive versus negative reinforcement methods) and the long-term success of the training. They found that using positive reinforcement, such as praise and food rewards, was much less likely to compromise the dog's welfare because it decreased anxiety. They also found that positive reinforcement was much more likely to reduce the number of dogs turned over to shelters when problematic behaviors were not being adequately corrected. The success rate of positive methods was quite evident in the success of the training.

Learning to live as a "good canine citizen" is paramount to a dog's safety as well as to his acceptance into the family household and community.

Positive dog training involves the use of rewards for good behavior—that is, performing the desired behavior, the behavior you are asking of your dog. The rewards can be food, praise, or positive actions such as petting or playing with a favorite toy. Try to figure out what motivates your dog. Havanese owners are quite fortunate because the breed as a whole becomes quite attached to their owners and is very willing to please.

HOW TO BEHAVE SO YOUR PUPPY BEHAVES

There are lots of games puppies play with each other that humans shouldn't participate in. Games such as keep away, tug of war, bite me, catch me, and the like will encourage behaviors that could become dangerous once your adorable puppy grows into a big and powerful adult—or into a feisty toy dog with a stubborn nature or a nasty bite. Keep-away might be cute when your pup is tiny and adorable, but as an adult, he might decide to play keep-away with your prescription bottle, your expensive sunglasses, or some other item of value or one that could potentially harm him. A tug of war game or one allowing your puppy to nip and bite can encourage aggression and other unacceptable behaviors, letting your dog assume a dominant position that could have serious consequences for both of you. Never play catch me. If your puppy gets loose outdoors and runs off, it can mean life or death if he doesn't come to you when you call him because he is used to running away from you and being rewarded for it.

So if your puppy tries to play any of these games, just pretend you have lost interest and turn away. Wait a few moments, and if he doesn't settle down then distract him with an acceptable game. Fetch is a good game that can also be used in training and in reinforcing basic commands. If he still doesn't settle down, disengage yourself from him, and as calmly as you can, leave the pup behind (in a safe, puppy-proof place). You only have to ignore him for a little while (less than 5 minutes, probably).

Be sure to always praise your puppy when he obeys and/or when he is playing nicely.

Socialization

Training begins with socialization. Socialization is the process of introducing your puppy to new things, people, and places, and helping him learn how to properly respond to them. Puppy socialization begins in the whelping box and occurs between the puppy's mom and the breeder, who spends time stroking and talking to the puppy.

Before any socialization or training can happen, however, your puppy must respect, trust, and have confidence in you. This means you must step up and take the role of his leader. If you do not, be assured your puppy will. Showering him with buckets of love and affection is the fun part of all this. Being firm and asserting leadership over him does not, however, mean bullying him or being dominant. Affection tempered with respect will result in a strong, loving bond between you and your puppy.

Early Training

By the time your Havanese pup is 8 weeks old, and extending to 12 weeks of age, he is exploring, tasting, licking, and chasing everything in sight. This is also a critical time at which all puppies go through a fear imprinting stage. However, a puppy's brain is more likely to accept new experiences at this time, making it an ideal period to begin teaching social skills and asserting your leadership.

Taking your puppy for walks is a great way to start socializing him. When people come up to pet him, ask them to approach him slowly and from the side; toy dogs really don't feel comfortable with someone towering over their heads. Being small, this is a first alert of possible danger. Also, do not socialize your puppy to large groups of dogs until he has been socialized to smaller

Socializing your puppy to a variety of new people, pets, and places ensures that he will become a confident and well-adjusted adult.

groups. Older dogs could easily find your puppy's antics beyond annoying. It is a mistake to think that all dogs will naturally like and take to one another. Use a leash to provide a protective environment for your puppy should another dog approach feeling territorial about his humans or his place. Be careful, however, not to let him sniff feces or other dogs because, at this age, his vaccine immunity isn't totally complete.

Try to avoid well-meaning but misguided attempts to soothe your puppy when he is frightened or anxious in response to an event, such as thunder and lightning. It is normal to become upset and anxious with loud crashing things. Trying to soothe your puppy rather than encouraging a "shake it off" attitude can result in inadvertently reinforcing negative behavior. I am less concerned about my puppies being frightened than I am in how well they recover. It is hard not to reach down to soothe an anxious puppy, but remember that the behavior you reinforce today is one you will live with for the next 10 to 12 years. So resist the urge to comfort your puppy and, rather, turn his attention to something positive such as a game, a snack, etc. Diversion and distraction tactics work quite well with Havanese.

To strengthen his obedience skills, consider taking your Havanese to puppy kindergarten beginning around the fourth month and/or when he has completed most of his inoculations.

Crate Training

I shudder when a potential puppy owner asks me if a puppy is crate trained or when they ask me to show them how to crate train. Inevitably, the next 10 to15 minutes is spent deciphering what they mean when referring to crate training: Do they think crate training means locking up the dog in a crate all day and only taking him out when they get home? Do they think crate training means using the crate to punish the dog? Do they think crate training is not necessary at all?

Let me begin by saying that crate training is necessary, and, when properly used, it offers an exceptional training tool. Crates also offer security and comfort. Dogs are den animals by nature, meaning that they will naturally seek a secluded space to retreat or withdraw to. Part of crate training is making sure your puppy sees his crate as a positive place.

How to Crate Train

Crate training is a gradual process. As with all things, you will need to guide your puppy so that he knows what to do. To get him used to going into his crate willingly, begin by choosing a command word, such as "crate." Whenever he enters it on his own, say the word "crate" and praise him. Place safe inedible toys or

Ask the Expert

CRATE TRAINING

Q: Why do I have to crate train my puppy?

A: Nancy Boyle is a breeder of champion Labrador Retrievers as well as Havanese. Her kennel, Heybern Showdogs, has produced champion field-tracking dogs, as well as champion companion dogs—her Havanese. Nancy asserts that crate training provides many worthwhile advantages. Although puppies do not like change any more than humans do, beginning this training soon after your new puppy arrives in your home will be the first step toward setting a firm foundation for his future learning and training, as well as offering him stability and some sense of security at a time when he is going through many adjustments. Here are her recommendations.

Your puppy should be brought home from the breeder in his crate, both for his safety and to make him feel less frightened during the trip. He should sleep in the crate at night beginning day one, preferably near you. Once he (eventually) falls asleep in the crate, don't say anything to him. If he awakens during the night crying, get him out, let him do his business, and then put him back in his crate. Don't turn on any lights; simply make it a quiet potty break, just as you would do if you woke up and needed to use the bathroom. Whenever you leave the house, always put him in his crate. However, never leave him there for very long. While he's still acclimating, always feed him in his crate so he identifies it with good things.

During the day, move the crate to an area of the house that involves lots of family activity (or keep another crate in that area). Never let your pup out of his crate as soon as you walk into the room. Ignore him and go about your business, make coffee, whatever. Let him out when you are ready. Don't get your pup wound up before opening the door. Getting let out of the crate should be a calm, matter-of-fact time; do not make it a very exciting event. Your pup should come to expect this as part of the daily routine, one in which you remain in charge. Crate training in this manner helps you to set boundaries and establish the first house rules your pup will need to follow to become a good family member. Dogs thrive on routine and settle in best when they know what's expected of them. And they rely on you for this much-needed guidance.

Puppies and dogs spend most of their day sleeping, and a crate is a great place to do this. It feels safe and secure, and it offers a dog private time, whether he goes there on his own or not. Most dogs eventually come to enjoy spending time in their crates and appreciate having a quiet space all their own.

—Nancy K. Boyle, Heybern Showdogs; Exhibitor, Breeder, Trainer.

chews (such as those manufactured by Nylabone) in the crate to provide him with something to play with and chew on. From time to time, drop a few pieces of kibble in the crate and play the game of "find the kibble." When he does, praise him, give him a treat, and repeat. Eventually, your puppy will want to enter the crate on his own.

Next, try giving the *crate* command, and praise your puppy if he enters. Once inside, offer him a treat as soon as he settles down. When he seems comfortable and reliable with this, try closing the crate door and walking away for only a few minutes. If he remains calm and doesn't whine, come back and open the door, but don't make a fuss over him. Practice this regularly, gradually extending the amount of time you stay away. He will soon like spending time in the crate and will often enter it on his own, seeking some quiet time or a nap.

Which approach to crate training you choose depends a great deal on your lifestyle. A new puppy will need to eliminate when he first awakens, after he eats, and after he plays. If you are at work all day, someone must come home during the day to let him out to potty and play. If that isn't possible, you may have to cordon off a spare room or an x-pen with newspapers or wee-wee pads at one end and food and water at the other end. An x-pen, or exercise pen, is a metal pen that closes off or encloses an area to safely contain a puppy. Of course, it's best not to leave a puppy alone for more than a few hours at a time.

How to Properly Use the Crate

When your Havanese first arrives, he will cry during the night to stay closer to his humans or to be taken out. I recommend that you place a crate near your bed. If the crying is just an "I'm lonesome and this is strange," cry, then just stick your hand through the door and wriggle your fingers so your puppy can smell you and be assured he's not alone. He should settle down quickly. If he keeps crying, he probably needs to go potty, so take him out with no detours and little talking. Show him that this is time to do his business. I recommend that food be given four hours before bed time and water two hours before bedtime.

During the day and evening, accustom your puppy to his crate by bringing it into common areas where the family spends a lot of time, such as the den or living room. In this way, he can feel part of the pack and not left out of family activities. When your puppy settles down, give him a small treat and praise him. If he seems to want too many treats, then just stick your fingers through the crate, wriggling them so he realizes he is not alone. Of course this should only be done for brief periods of time during crate training. Your puppy should otherwise be out of his crate and spending time with you when you are at home to supervise him.

Rules of Use

Except for during the night, puppies should not be crated for longer than 6 hours maximum. The following is a guide showing the length of time a puppy should be crated relative to his age.

There is a difference between using a crate as punishment (which *never* should be done) and providing the crate as a time out. Even puppies need sufficient daily exercise, and a lack of this might result in unwanted behaviors such as excessive rowdiness or nipping. Do not allow your children to get in the crate with your dog or to handle the puppy while he's in his crate.

Housetraining

Housetraining refers to teaching your Havanese puppy the appropriate place to eliminate. By nature, dogs love their dens and do not want to eliminate in them, so housetraining accidents will not often happen in the crate if it is properly used. However, your puppy will need to be shown where he can and shouldn't eliminate.

Potty Schedule

Puppies usually must use the bathroom:
- right after waking up
- after a few moments of excited play
- after eating
- after drinking
- a few hours after the last potty break

Generally, a puppy's elimination schedule is one hour for each month of age plus one. In other words, a 2-month-old puppy can hold his bladder and bowels for 3 hours, a 3-month-old for 4 hours, a 5-month-old for 6 hours, etc. Many puppies cannot be fully housetrained before they are 6 months old. By that age, they can "hold it" for up to 7 hours.

CRATING DURATION GUIDELINES

9 to 10 weeks	approximately 30 to 60 minutes
11 to 14 weeks	approximately 1 to 3 hours
15 to 16 weeks	approximately 3 to 4 hours
17+ weeks	approximately 4 to 6 hours maximum

Pay attention to when and what your puppy is doing, in general, before he has to potty. This would include after sleeping, playing, and eating, and whatever particular behaviors (subtle signs such as sniffing, circling, breaking from play or interacting) he shows before he goes. Be prepared to take your puppy to his potty area immediately at these times or whenever he shows signs of needing to go.

How to Prevent Accidents

Set up a place where you want your puppy to potty (e.g., a bathroom or laundry room layered with newspaper, a spot in the back yard, etc.). Do not permit him unsupervised freedom in areas where you do not want him to potty. If your puppy doesn't go to the bathroom in the potty area, take him back to his crate or bed or to the newspaper-covered "safe" area, and try again in another 30 to 60 minutes. In this way, you establish a set routine for your puppy, showing him that when he goes to the bathroom in the right place he gets rewarded. It also helps lessen the possibility of his making a mistake and going in the wrong place. Your puppy will learn that it's really worth his while to eliminate outside, and that inside, the carpets are a place for fun and games he can only access if he doesn't have accidents there.

Immediately after your puppy has eliminated, you can usually consider him "empty" and therefore safe to leave on your carpet or furniture until you encounter one of the conditions listed above. If your puppy has not yet emptied his bladder, do not let him have access to areas in which you want to avoid accidents. Only leave him in a crate or bed where his natural instincts will prevent him from soiling his area, encouraging him to hold it until he gets to his potty place. Or, place him in a location where it's all right if he eliminates (like in an x-pen, or in a room with a newspaper-covered floor, or outside). Otherwise, you must watch him closely. "Watching him closely" means he doesn't have a chance to go when you're not looking.

How to Handle Accidents

What if your puppy makes a mistake? If you follow basic housetraining rules, you won't often discover a nasty wet spot or a smelly surprise. But if you catch your puppy in the act, or if you see him sniffing or squatting and about to act, try to interrupt (not scold) him by saying "No." Quickly pick him up (if possible!) and immediately take him outside or to his indoor potty area. Put him down, and watch him. As soon as he goes there, praise him. Then properly clean up the accident with enzymatic cleaner.

Never scold or punish your puppy for going to the bathroom in the wrong place. He won't understand it. Dogs don't

When housetraining your Havanese, choose a spot in your yard where you want him to eliminate, and take him to that same area every time.

understand pointing and yelling, and they won't remember your reprimand and associate it with the accident later on. They will only learn that it's not safe to go to the bathroom in front of you, or to be near you when you're near "their toilet area." Likewise, rubbing a dog's nose in it will only teach him to avoid you, as will slapping him with a newspaper or rattling a metal can with pennies in it and startling him when he's going.

Basic Obedience Training

Basic obedience training is not difficult, and it can be done for short periods of time each day. First, you'll need to identify a set of commands, or cue words, you want to use. I recommend the basic commands that you will use every day, ones that can also be really life-saving commands. These are: *sit, come, stay, down,* and *heel.*

When you give your dog a command, it is important to reward him quickly. Dogs—and particularly puppies—have only about a 5-second window of concentration opportunity that you need to take advantage of. They also have

CHECKLIST: GOOD CANINE CITIZEN OBJECTIVES

The purpose of the American Kennel Club's (AKC)'s Canine Good Citizen (CGC) program is to promote responsible dog guardianship and to encourage well-behaved dogs who are welcome in the home and community. If a dog properly performs all ten objectives required by the CGC program test, he is awarded a certificate and a tag designating him a good canine citizen. It is up to you whether you want your dog to take part in this course. Some activities and sports will require a CGC certificate, as will some places in which you live. It's advisable to take the training class to prepare for the exam, but you don't have to. The following behaviors are expected at the CGC test.

✓ **Meeting friendly new people:** Your dog will be expected to sit or stand calmly while you stop and speak to a stranger.

✓ **A pat on the head:** Your dog must sit or stand calmly while a stranger pets him.

✓ **A trip to the veterinarian/groomer:** Your dog must permit a stranger to brush him and examine his paws and ears.

✓ **A walk in the park:** Your dog will be asked to walk with you on a loose leash, including turning left, right, and around, and coming to a stop.

✓ **A walk in a crowd:** Your dog must show he is at ease while you walk him in a crowd.

✓ **Staying put:** Your dog must perform a sit and/or down and then remain in place while you walk away from him.

✓ **Answering a call:** Your dog must come when you command.

✓ **Dog to dog:** When meeting another dog, your dog must show only casual interest.

✓ **Accepting the unexpected:** Your dog must not panic when confronted by common distractions, such as a loud noise or a passing jogger.

✓ **Dog-sitters welcome:** Your dog should behave when a friendly stranger takes his leash and you disappear for three minutes.

It's fun to try these ten criteria to see how many behaviors your dog could properly perform. For more information about the CGC program, visit www.akc.org.

limited retention, so the command needs to be practiced several times a day. Three issues in positive reinforcement training are consistency, timing, and persistence. It is also advisable to choose a time when it is not hectic, when you and puppy can concentrate on the work to be done.

Sit

The *sit* command is one of the easiest to teach and learn. Additionally, it sets the foundation for the *stay* and *down* commands.

To teach the *sit*:

1. Show your puppy that you have a treat in your hand. Next, hold the treat just above his nose; too high and he will jump up to get it, which you don't want to happen.
2. Call your puppy's name in a firm voice, and then give the *sit* command while you slowly move the treat over his head and between his ears. Your dog will follow the treat, which will move him into a sit position.
3. When your puppy's rear touches the ground, say "good sit" and give him the treat, followed by petting and praising.

Come

Come is one of the most frustrating commands for your puppy to learn, but a very important one.

To teach the *come*:

1. First, load up on your puppy's favorite treats.
2. For safety, begin training this command in the house. Call your puppy's name, and when he comes and stands at your feet, give him a treat.
3. Repeat this constantly, until he will come when he hears your voice and is focused on something else.
4. When he is reliable, take him outside to a secure area. Repeat the exercise you practiced indoors. Call your puppy's name. When he raises his head, praise him, and when he comes and stands at your feet, give him his treat.

Repeat this exercise all the time.

Stay

The *stay* command is just as important in protecting your puppy as the *come* command. A successful *stay* occurs when your puppy does not move from his current position.

To teach the *stay*:

1. Get your puppy into a sitting position, then praise and treat him.
2. Next, say his name, followed by "stay," as you back up a step or two. Your puppy should remain in position. If not, put him back into a sit and begin again.
3. Once he holds the sit for a second or two, give a release command, such as "okay."
4. Repeat this exercise several times a day, moving farther away from your puppy with each practice. Start with 1- to 2-second periods of staying, and work up to several minutes until your puppy performs it reliably. Then use it in everyday situations.

Down

Teaching the *down* command is almost as easy as teaching the *sit* command. The down is a very useful command, especially in calming an overexcited puppy. It's also useful in keeping your puppy calm when greeting and talking with someone, or if you will be doing something for an extended period of time and need your puppy to remain nearby.

To teach the *down*:

1. Call your puppy's name and show him you have a treat in your hand.
2. Next, place the treat above his nose as you do when training the *sit* command, but this time move it slowly toward the floor (not over his head). Once near the floor, draw it slowly toward you so that your puppy stretches out toward it.
3. When his hocks and elbows are on the floor, say "good down" and give him the treat.
4. Repeat this exercise until your puppy performs it reliably. Then use it in everyday situations.

Heel

The *heel* command teaches your puppy to walk nicely on leash.

To teach the *heel*:

1. First, you will need some treats, a flat-buckle collar sized for a puppy, and a 15-foot (38-cm) cotton training leash. You'll also need to practice in a location large enough for you to walk around at random, as well as one that has a few distractions (i.e., other puppies and dogs, children, noises, etc.).
2. To begin, hold the cotton training leash in both hands in front of your waist, and allow your puppy to walk in any directions he chooses so he can become accustomed to walking on leash. Do this a few times over a period of days until he seems comfortable.
3. Once your puppy's adjusted to being leashed, let him have the lead and follow his nose. Dogs are sensitive to the pressure of a leash, so maintain slight tension on it at all times. However, it shouldn't be taut or completely loose.
4. If your puppy starts to pull or stray from your side, simply stop moving.
5. When he responds by stopping, immediately make eye contact, say "good heel," and reward his correct behavior with praise and a treat.
6. Then continue walking. If he begins to pull or stray again, repeat the previous steps.
7. Repeat this exercise until your puppy performs it reliably. Eventually, he will walk nicely on leash, relying on you for guidance.

An enjoyable side effect of learning basic commands is that you and your puppy may decide to take a step further and explore more advanced obedience training. If you do well, agility, flyball, and rally obedience are a few of the more popular performance sports in which you and your Havanese can participate, offering exercise, a chance to have fun, and opportunities to strengthen the bond you share.

FINDING A TRAINER

When asked what the most important thing a person should look for when considering hiring a professional dog trainer, Billy Akins, owner and founder of Sandy Hills Kennel and a certified trainer replied, "Love! The trainer has to love—and I mean *really* love—dogs." But that would be a bit difficult to know until you meet the trainer. In general, a good trainer should be certified, adaptable, and love dogs.

First, do some homework about the Havanese breed—learn about its temperament and its trainability. Havanese are eager to please their people, so a heavy hand in training is not necessary—and can have negative consequences. Make sure that the trainer and her methods suit the Havanese breed. You would not want to hire a trainer who specializes in only training police or military dogs, for instance. And you never want to hire one who openly advocates negative or harsh correction-based methods. Ideally, you want to find one who has worked with toy breeds.

You may want to ask your vet or breeder for recommendations. Once you find a few good candidates in your area, ask if the trainer is certified and if you can have or see a copy of the certification. Visit the grounds of the training facility to be sure they are safe. Is the training area properly secured? Are there enough staff members on hand to attend to all the dogs? Does the trainer have control of the dogs during class? Does she mix really large and nervous dogs with smaller companion dogs during the training session? Do the dogs and owners seem to respond well to the trainer? If you are not comfortable with any aspect of the class or environment, interview a few more trainers.

Training programs offered through your local kennel club are a good place to look for trainers. However, these trainers are usually volunteers of the kennel club who are either judges or are showing their own dogs, so their schedules might be difficult to fit into yours. Some trainers offer private in-home services and will come to your home to help you train your dog. The first visit is usually spent teaching you and other family members how to work with your new puppy. It is really important that members of the household are consistent in using commands and adhering to house rules.

Training is well worth the effort—a well-behaved dog is not only a pleasure to live with and love, but he's also a happy, confident, and loyal life-long companion.

Chapter
7

Solving Problems With Your Havanese

As mentioned in Chapter 6, all kinds of behaviors occur when puppies interact with their humans, and some of these behaviors may be inappropriate or difficult for us to deal with in daily life with our pets. Nipping, herding, jumping, chewing, digging, and house soiling are some problems you may encounter. So why do puppies do these things? They are so cute, right?

Well, there are several things that puppy problem behaviors have in common. First is a failure of the human to establish her leadership role, which should be clear from the moment puppy lands in his new home. At the end of the day, a dog is a pack animal who requires your leadership. Now, this does not mean that you have to be big and authoritarian, nor does it mean engaging in a battle of wills. It does mean possessing an air of authority. This is not new to a Havanese puppy, whose mother backs off around 5 weeks of age, when puppy teeth make nursing painful. She returns around the eighth to ninth week and begins teaching her offspring the rules of engagement.

I have seen a Havanese mother clear across the room from her puppy, who is

Once the root causes of problem behaviors are identified, they can usually be managed or eliminated. Most are caused by boredom, lack of sufficient exercise, stress, or fear.

paying her no mind and happily engaged in typical pushy puppy behavior with his siblings or toys, make a beeline run at him, knock him over, and pin him to the floor until he stops hollering and growling. If he manages to slip away from her, she will repeat the behavior. Now lest you think this is so awful, look again in about ten minutes, when the puppy is doing something his mom approves of, and listen for her high-pitched yelps of approval, accompanied by licking, kissing, and grooming. Both amble off into the canine sunset until it's time to teach the next rule.

So with all this in mind, how do you go about establishing yourself as your dog's leader in a positive way? It isn't as difficult as you may think because most dogs are eager to please—every dog needs a leader to listen to, obey, and please. In nature, dogs constantly make decisions and modify their behavior based on their changing circumstances so that they can seek out the best possible outcome. You can use this natural instinct to reinforce the behaviors you prefer and set the house rules. Dogs are motivated by the anticipation of a reward or the desire to avoid something unpleasant. So to be effective, training has to be consistent and positive: Your dog should expect a positive response (such as a treat, praise, or a even just a pat on the head) from you—his pack leader—every time

he performs the behavior you want. As a result, he will willingly modify his natural instincts—the ones that may be bothersome to you—and make more acceptable behavioral choices while looking for your approval.

By using positive training methods, you also can modify or manage problem behaviors or teach entirely new behaviors, ranging from basic good manners to advanced obedience. Dogs need boundaries and structure to understand what you want and what is expected of them. Most problem behaviors are caused by a lack of structure and guidance, which are the owner's responsibility to give. It would be truly unfair to expect your dog to behave without giving him the opportunity to learn the house rules so that he can live successfully with his family pack. Consistent, fair, and loving training will keep both you and your dog happy.

Barking

The first thing you must come to terms with is that new puppies will cry from time to time, especially if they have changed their living quarters. Havanese are not barkers in the sense that other breeds are considered nuisance barkers. Havanese are more "notifying barkers," meaning that they are keen to let their owners know when someone approaches their territory. Once the leader of the

THE IMPORTANCE OF A SCHEDULE
FOR BEHAVIOR CONTROL

The consistency of a schedule can really help prevent problem behaviors because your puppy will gain confidence, feel safe, and always know what to expect. Here's what an ideal routine looks like:

7:00-7:30 a.m.: Wake up and go for a brisk walk; this also gives your puppy an opportunity to urinate and defecate. If you have 10 minutes for a little playtime, that would be great; fetch or another simple interactive game is fine. Spend about 10 minutes of quality time just talking to and petting your dog. After your puppy has eliminated, take him back into the house.

7:30-8:00 a.m.: Time to eat breakfast. Offer fresh food and water in clean bowls. Pick up any uneaten portions after 20 minutes and refrigerate them for later in the day.

8:00-9:00 a.m.: Dogs need to go out after they eat so they can urinate and defecate. Ideally, most dogs would enjoy some interaction again, with the opportunity to exercise or play.

9:00–12 noon: Nap time. Or, in the case of Havanese, time to follow you around as you go about your day. If you are off to work, then nap time may be followed by play time. Be sure to leave toys and chews to keep your dog entertained while you are gone.

12:00–1:00 p.m.: Give your dog another opportunity to exercise, play, and eliminate. If you have a puppy, feed him his lunchtime meal. Offer fresh food and water. Pick up any uneaten portions after 20 minutes and remove the bowl.

1:00–5:00 p.m.: Nap time again. Or, another opportunity to keep you company while you go about your daily chores.

5:00–7:30 p.m.: Dinner time, followed by lots of play time! Offer fresh food and water. Monitor your dog's appetite. Offer a longer and more extensive play time than you did in the morning. Let your dog play vigorously and burn off some of that pent-up energy. A tired dog is a happy dog.

7:30–11:00 p.m.: Quiet family time. This may be a good opportunity to brush and groom you dog, brush his teeth, and spend some quality time together on the couch watching some television or reading. Before bed time, take your dog out to potty one last time. Then tuck him in with a big hug.

pack (that's you!) lets them know that everything is okay, they settle down.

How to Manage It

When you let your dog out of his crate after returning home, make sure that he is not barking when you do so. If he's barking, do not pay attention to him. Go about putting your keys away, checking the mail, and getting supper ready. Once he has quieted down, open the door and let him out. Praise and treat him for his good behavior.

In other situations, you can train a no bark command, although this can be one of the more challenging commands because you must catch your puppy in the act and reward him when he is not barking.

To stop excessive barking, teach your dog to bark on command. Say "speak" and knock on a hard surface to get him to begin barking. When he stops, immediately say "no bark" and reward him with a treat. This teaches him that bringing a noise to your attention is acceptable, but continued barking is not.

You can also train your dog to stop barking by interrupting it as soon as it starts. When your dog starts to bark, call him, ask him to sit, throw a ball, or give him a chew toy to keep his mouth occupied. If you notice that specific things constantly prompt barking, like the arrival of the mailman, systematically interrupt

him as soon as he starts and reward him for being quiet.

Chewing

Destructive chewing is not only a sign of boredom—it's also a sign that your puppy may be cutting his permanent canines, which usually occurs at around 4 months of age. You may not realize it until you find a baby tooth somewhere. I can only think how uncomfortable this is for the puppy!

How to Manage It

First, if your puppy is teething, find something appropriate that he can chew on and put it in his crate. It can be either an edible or inedible chew, such as those made by Nylabone for puppies. You may, from time to time, even cover a piece of ice in a washcloth and rub it on his gums to ease the soreness.

This strategy also applies to adults. Rather than trying to discourage your dog from chewing, redirect his chewing to suitable objects. Whenever you discover your dog chewing something he shouldn't have, remove the item from his mouth and trade it for an acceptable chew toy. Keep plenty of great chew toys on hand for him. However, don't make them all available at once. Rotating the toys will maintain his interest in them.

If your dog is chewing out of boredom, he may not be getting enough exercise

DOG-PROOFING YOUR HOME

Dog-proofing your home and yard will not only keep your Havanese out of trouble, but it is essential to his safety and well-being. Here are some basics:

- Secure all electrical cords and keep them out of reach. They can either be taped to the wall or placed inside a piece of flexible plumbing pipe.
- Keep windows and doors closed, and block access to off-limits areas with safety gates. Upper-story windows, in particular, should be kept closed and free of any aids to exiting them (e.g., chairs or other items that help a dog climb up to the window, etc.).
- Keep all household cleaners out of reach.
- Keep the toilet bowl lid down. Toilet bowl cleaners are strongly alkaline and caustic.
- Keep medication bottles out of reach. An insistent dog can get through a child-proof cap quickly.
- Dispose of bones (especially poultry bones) in a dog-proof manner. I wrap mine twice in plastic grocery bags before stowing them in our garbage cans.
- Prevent any choking hazards by keeping small items such as buttons, needles, pins, string, and the like put away.
- Keep all chemicals stored in the garage and out of reach. For example, antifreeze is highly toxic and has a sweet smell that is strongly attractive to dogs. Garden pesticides and rodent poisons should be used carefully and not in areas to which your dog has access.
- Keep cigarettes, which are toxic to dogs, and ashtrays where your dog cannot reach them.
- Keep your dog away from toxic human foods, such as chocolate, grapes, onions, and garlic. You can find a list on the ASPCA's website at www.aspca.org.
- Keep your dog away from toxic plants, both indoors and outdoors. You can find a list on the ASPCA's website at aspca.org.
- Christmas decorations should be kept out of your dog's reach. An alternative is to place an x-pen or playpen around the Christmas tree.
- Do not burn candles where they are accessible to dogs, and always remember to use your fire screen when enjoying a winter fire.

and/or is being left alone for too long. Play with your dog regularly and provide him with a wide variety of interesting chew toys to prevent him from getting bored in your absence. You might also consider using a doggy day care two to three times a week, as a way of increasing your dog's socialization.

Occasionally, destructive chewing might be related to separation anxiety, a behavior rooted in a dog's anxiety over being left by the human he has bonded to; this excessive bonding is sometimes called hyperattachment. However, there is a growing concern that separation anxiety is being misidentified. Destructive behavior may be a result of separation anxiety, but it could just be normal puppy behavior, play, reaction to outside stimuli, and/or an outlet for excess energy. First, have your puppy assessed by your veterinarian. She is the one to determine (based on what you tell her) if the source of the destructive behavior is medical or behavioral. If she thinks that separation anxiety is the cause of the destructive behavior, she might recommend that you see a behaviorist or she may prescribe medication. If, however, the destructive behavior does not seem due to separation anxiety, you will have to identify what has changed to cause your dog to break his training. Often this requires going back to the beginning and reteaching training basics.

Rather than trying to discourage your dog from chewing, redirect the behavior to suitable objects, such as safe chew toys.

To help control destructive chewing, try spraying bitter apple or bitter lemon on those things you don't want your Havanese to chew. These sprays can help, but are best used in conjunction with the behavior altering methods described above.

Digging

Havanese are not diggers in the way that some terrier breeds are, but they can and will dig from time to time. Some dogs dig because it is ingrained in their ancestry— it is their job to follow a scent and seek out vermin. Others dig because they are hot and trying to make a cool hole to lie in, or because they are trying to escape confinement. Digging may also be the result of lack of exercise, loneliness, or boredom. If you can find the reason for your dog's digging, then you can usually find a solution.

How to Manage It

The easiest way to prevent digging is to supervise your dog when he is outdoors. Section off a small part of the yard where he's allowed to dig to his heart's content, or make a doggy "sandbox" filled with loose dirt or sand. When you catch your dog digging in the yard or garden, give the command "No!" in a firm voice and lead him quickly to his digging spot. When he digs in this area, encourage him with a special command like "dig" followed by praise.

Also make sure your dog is getting enough exercise. Give him adequate daily opportunities to participate in activities he enjoys. Brisk daily walks, play sessions, or a romp in the yard or park are just fine.

If you must leave your dog outside in the yard for a fairly long time, be sure he has things to amuse himself with, such as safe chew toys and bones, or food dispensing toys that he has to manipulate to dispense the treat. It's important to keep your dog mentally and physically stimulated.

House Soiling

There are several reasons for a housetrained puppy or dog to begin house soiling. Inappropriate elimination can be due to medical or behavioral causes.

How to Manage It

If your dog has suddenly begun house soiling, first check to see if there is a medical reason. For example, a urinary tract infection, especially in a puppy, can really cause loss of bladder control. If your dog is eliminating feces in the house, that too might be indicative of a medical problem. Parasites can cause him to begin house soiling when he had otherwise been quite reliable. Impacted anal glands can also cause changes in stool habits. Your vet can examine your dog to identify or eliminate possible causes. If medication is required, be sure you give it accurately and on time.

If you find your dog digging in your flowers, give him his own digging area.

Once medical reasons have been ruled out, consider behavioral causes. First to come to mind is that the puppy or dog was not adequately housetrained in the first place, which may include inadequate crate training as well. At this point, I recommend retraining your dog in both housetraining and crate training, starting at the beginning again if necessary. (See Chapter 6.) Clearly, your dog is not ready for so much freedom in the house, and he needs a basic refresher course. Additionally, reevaluate your feeding schedule. Dogs who are free-fed will have a more difficult time controlling their bowels and bladder than will those fed on a schedule.

Consistent supervision is the key to successfully housetraining your dog. If you cannot keep an eye on him at all times, get some cotton cording (or a long leash) and tie one end to your waist and the other to your Havanese's collar. The cotton cording should be no longer than 8 feet (2.5 m). This will give you an opportunity to more closely supervise

GAMES WITH YOUR PUPPY

Q: I've heard that certain games encourage problem behaviors in some dogs. What are the best games to play with a puppy?

A: There are lots of games that puppies play with each other that humans shouldn't play with them, such as keep-away and tug-of-war. Keep-away might be cute at this age, but as an adult, your puppy might decide to play keep-away with your prescription bottle, your expensive sunglasses, or something else. The same goes for tug-of-war. So at this age, if he tries to play any of these games, just pretend that you have lost interest and turn away. Catch-me is also a very important game to never play. If your puppy gets loose outside some day, it can mean life or death because he needs to know that he should always come to you when you call, not run away. So inside, where it's safe, turn around and ignore your puppy if he starts to playfully run away when you call him.

—Nancy K. Boyle, Heybern Showdogs; Exhibitor, Breeder, Trainer.

signs that he needs to potty.

If your dog is having accidents indoors, an enzymatic cleanser is essential in helping remove all traces of odor, which dogs can smell even when you think the area is clean. If you'd like to use a more natural remedy, fill a squirt bottle half with water and half with white distilled vinegar. As always when using products on fabric, test an obscure corner for colorfastness first.

Jumping Up

It is hard not to be beguiled by the Havanese's jumping acrobatics, especially when he dances and twirls for you—the breed has an amazing vertical jump for such a little dog! However, as your dog gets older, this will become less charming as clothing is torn, arms are scratched, and tempers flare.

So why do Havanese jump like that? Part of the answer is because they can, and because their small size seems anatomically constructed to make it possible. In addition, they like to jump up when they're excited, especially when guests arrive at the house.

How to Manage It

To keep your dog from jumping up on you or your guests, use the sit and stay commands, combined with a hand gesture of your choosing, as people enter your home. Having your dog sit, stay, and wait to be greeted by strangers is one of the best ways to prevent jumping up.

We have multiple dogs, so training them not to jump and possibly bolt out of an open door is critical to their safety. Proper door manners—sitting and waiting at the door—are not difficult to teach if approached with consistency and patience on the part of all family members. (I have two Havanese females who love to ride in my truck and who will jump on me, then sneak around my feet to get past me to the door. Amazingly, the other Havanese all sit in a circle and watch me go through the routine of leaving. Clearly, the two girls are going to need additional training.)

Nipping and Herding

Nipping and herding seem to go hand in hand with the Havanese. As you are walking, you may find that your puppy is behind you, head butting your legs

Having your dog sit, stay, and wait to be greeted by strangers is one of the best ways to prevent jumping up.

or nipping you fairly painfully. Usually, this occurs in a case of high excitement, such as during food preparation, when you're leaving the house, or perhaps when children are darting by.

The controversy continues on whether or not Havanese were used to herd poultry in Cuba. Some Havanese, notably at breeder Suzanne McKay's Mimosa kennel, have been trained to herd, and they have earned Herding Trial ribbons herding both ducks and sheep. McKay makes the point, however, that it is unlikely that the Havanese's aristocratic owners would allow their beloved little dog to indulge in such dirty barnyard games, but this does not negate the fact that Havanese are highly trainable as herding dogs.

Mouthing behavior occurs when your puppy decides that your arm or hand is his new chew toy. While most Havanese have what we call a "soft mouth," meaning that he just mouths without biting or nipping, it is not a behavior to leave uncorrected. As your puppy grows, this soft mouth can become a hard and dangerous mouth.

How to Manage It

When your puppy nips you, let out a loud yelp and put the puppy in his crate for no longer than five minutes. During this time, go on about your business while ignoring the puppy. Take him out only if he is quiet and settled down. Alternatively, replace whatever body part is being nipped with any good distraction mechanism, such as finding him something appropriate he can chew on.

When you are being herded and nipped in the rear, stop. Raise your foot with the sole side facing the dog and start walking backward (without tripping over him, of course!) while emitting a loud yelp. This may take a couple of tries, but your dog should eventually stop trying to herd you. Then, ignore your puppy until he settles down. Another technique is to carry a treat or food in front of you as you walk and refuse to put it down until your puppy has settled.

When to Seek Professional Help

If you feel you have tried every approach possible, including obedience classes, and are still unable to manage a problem behavior, it may be time to seek the services of a professional. This is especially important in cases of aggression and separation anxiety. Dogs labeled biters are impossible to place in rescue because of liability issues, and they are often euthanized. So before that step is reached, be sure that you have a good conversation with your vet.

Your vet may do two things: Put your dog on medication and/or recommend an animal behaviorist. A trained animal

Check It Out

PROBLEM BEHAVIOR CHECKLIST

✓ Develop a daily schedule that meshes with puppy's life with humans.

✓ Establish yourself as the leader of your doggy–human pack to help prevent problem behaviors.

✓ Prevent destructive chewing by providing inedible and edible chews.

✓ Deal with digging by supervising your Havanese closely or even giving him his own area in which to dig.

✓ Remember that house soiling is not normal and can have both medical and behavioral causes. If an accident occurs (and it will), use an enzymatic cleaner to eliminate the odor, which will draw the puppy to the area again.

✓ If your puppy bites or nips, check to see if he is bored or not feeling well.

✓ Eliminate jumping behavior by asking your Havanese to sit and stay when guests arrive at the door.

behaviorist can offer solutions to serious problems, such as aggression, phobias, and obsessive behavior, and design a program that you can continue to implement at home. She will interview you about your dog's problem, observe him in your home, and interpret the causes of his inappropriate actions based on training and experience. She also may consult with your veterinarian to rule out any medical issues that may be causing or contributing to the problem, and she will work with the vet to devise a program that includes medication.

Although the field of animal behavior science has become quite professionalized, there are still some charlatans out there, so depend on your vet to make a recommendation for you. A certified animal behaviorist (CAAB) or a board-certified veterinary behaviorist (Dip ACVB) has degrees in animal behavior, psychology, biology, zoology, veterinary medicine, and other related disciplines. You can get reliable referrals from the following organizations:

• National Association of Animal Behaviorists (NAAB) at www. animalbehaviorists.org

• International Association of Animal Behavior Consultants, Inc. (IAABC) at www.iaabc.org

Chapter
8

**Activities With
Your Havanese**

Few things bond a Havanese to his owner more securely than doing something together. While daily walks are pleasurable, structured activities such as obedience, agility, tracking, and rally bring another level of bonding and enjoyment. Havanese are little dogs who enjoy learning new tricks, commands, and activities. I don't know if this is specific to Havanese only or to intelligent dogs in general, but certainly, the Havanese seems to eagerly embrace learning new things.

Sports and Activities

There are an increasing number of activities and organized sports in which dogs and their owners may participate and compete. Canine competitive events offer various types of training classes to meet the requirements for different levels of competition.

Canine Good Citizen Program

The Canine Good Citizen (CGC) training program is a certificate program that is open to every dog. While it may be taught as part of a puppy class, the instructor must be an American Kennel Club (AKC) CGC certified instructor. Your dog must know the basic commands to earn a CGC title. Often, this is a first necessary step to becoming a therapy dog.

Obedience

Obedience training and competition is the oldest and most fundamental of the canine companion activities. Both dog and handler are assessed on how well they (theoretically) meet whatever image the judge has of a perfect dog while he executes a series of commands. Accommodations for the jumps, rings, and dumbbells are made for toy breeds, thus allowing Havanese to compete. The extremely strong urge of the Havanese to please his owner and learn new commands makes him especially well suited to obedience competition.

Levels of competition in obedience trials include Novice, Open, and Utility, each with increasing degrees of difficulty. Skill sets for each level are based on obedience skills such as heeling on and off lead, staying in both a sit and a down position with a group of dogs, coming when called, and standing for a simple examination.

The Companion Dog (CD) title is earned at the Novice level and reflects the Havanese's aptitude at a series of basic obedience command exercises. The Companion Dog Excellent (CDX) title exercises build upon the basic commands at the Novice level, but the dog performs each exercise for longer periods of time. The Utility Dog (UD) title exercises are performed using only hand signals, plus the dog must also retrieve a dumbbell, pick up a glove, and jump through a hoop.

Puppy Love

SOCIALIZATION THROUGH SPORTS AND ACTIVITIES

A Havanese puppy does best in all aspects of life when he is well socialized—whether during daily interactions or while participating in activities and sports. Breeders have already begun the socialization process while the puppies are with them during their first few months of life. At the breeding kennel, they live with their mom and littermates, as well as with other Havanese of all sizes and types. The puppies have been groomed a couple of times, complete with bathing and teeth brushing. They have traveled in a crate to the vet on several occasions. Most importantly, they have been handled by a variety of humans and other dogs. When socialization is continued in puppy training, competitions, sports, traveling, or therapy dog work, your Havanese puppy will grow more familiar and comfortable with the world in which he is growing up and lives. And a busy and active puppy is a happy one!

Agility

GRCH Ch. Tejano's Eye of the Storm RN NAJ aka Sky is a champion Havanese sometimes referred to as a "double-handled dog," meaning he has titles at both ends of his name. After he won his conformation titles (Champion and Grand Champion), he began competing in agility and proved again that talent in one area doesn't preclude talent in another.

Agility competition is one of the fastest-growing events since the first agility trial was held by the AKC in 1994. Agility has three levels of classes. The first is Standard, which consists of a timed obstacle course that includes a dog walk, seesaw, and A-frame. The dog must run 15 to 20 stations on a timed course. Both verbal commands and hand signals may be used.

The second class is Jumpers and Weaves. It consists of tunnels, jumps, and weave poles. The third class is Fifteen and Send Time, or FAST, in which Havanese can particularly shine, given the level of their innate intelligence, because it requires strategic skill, speed, accuracy, and distance handling. After winning an Excellent Standard title and an Excellent Jumpers title, the dog and handler can compete for the Master Agility Championship (MACH) title.

Sky has certainly demonstrated that Havanese are well suited to agility. Since he led the way, the numbers of Havanese competing in agility trials have grown.

Rally

Rally is the newest of the AKC's titling

competitions. With its roots in obedience trials, this sport was devised specifically with the pet owner in mind because both dog and handler can compete at their own pace. In addition to their small size, speed, and cognitive power, Havanese have an ability to stop short and to interpret commands rapidly, making them ideal candidates for rally competition.

Custom designed by a judge at each event, a rally course averages 10 to 20 stations. Each station has a sign providing

Canine freestyle, for which the Havanese is ideally suited, incorporates a mixture of obedience, dancing, and tricks.

instructions regarding the next skill that is to be performed. Scoring is not as rigorous as in traditional obedience.

The different levels of rally increase in complexity of commands and ability to work off leash. The three levels of competition include Novice, Advanced, and Excellent. The Novice-level exercises are performed with the leash on, and handlers are allowed to give verbal commands and encouragement. Advanced-level exercises are all performed off leash and consist of 12 to 17 stations. The Excellent-level exercises are the most challenging. They consist of 15 to 20 stations, with all work performed off leash and only verbal encouragement used. To receive a rally title, three qualifying scores under two different judges must be obtained.

Canine Freestyle

Canine freestyle incorporates a mixture of obedience, dancing, and tricks. This results in an activity that offers perhaps the highest level of interaction between owner and dog.

There are two varieties of the sport: musical freestyle and freestyle heeling, also known as heelwork to music. The difference between the two varieties is that freestyle heeling focuses on a dog's ability to stay in variations of the heel position while the handler moves to music. As an athletic toy dog with acrobatic abilities, the Havanese is an ideal candidate for freestyle.

Conformation

Conformation dog shows are designed to assess AKC-registered breeding stock by evaluating how well the overall appearance and structure of the dog meets his breed standard. The standard provides a detailed description of what the perfect breed specimen should look like.

The three types of conformation dog shows are all-breed shows, which are open to the over 150 breeds and are the shows most frequently seen on television; specialty shows, which are restricted to the showing of one breed (for example, the annual Havanese Club of America National Specialty shows only Havanese); and group shows, which are open only to specific dog groups: sporting, hounds, working, herding, terrier, non-sporting, and toy. Spayed or neutered dogs may not enter conformation shows since that would defeat the purpose of the competition, which is to assess breeding stock. To earn a conformation championship, a dog must garner 15 points, with two major wins under two different judges.

The most prestigious conformation competition is the Best of Breed Show, in which the winners of each of the dog groups compete for the Best of Breed championship title. Winners of this title are eligible to compete in the highly esteemed Westminster Kennel Club (WKC) dog show. Havanese were first eligible to be shown in 2000. Ch. Los Perritos Laredo was awarded Best of Breed (BOB) at the Westminster Kennel Club and the AKC Eukanuba competitions in 2005. The Havanese won its first Group 3 placement in 2008. That same year, Ch. Los Perritos Wee Pantaloons aka Pan was awarded top-producing toy dog.

Participation in conformation shows can occur simply at the spectator level, as something you and your dog enjoy. It can also occur on the more active level if you decide that you want to show your Havanese. The AKC has some wonderful information on beginning to show your dog, which you can find online at www.akc.org/events/conformation/beginners.cfm. Finding an experienced mentor is also a good idea. The best place to find one is to join a local kennel club. The AKC, which is the club of clubs, keeps a list of local clubs on its website as well.

Therapy Work

The Havanese' s high level of empathic intelligence makes him uniquely suited for therapy work. However, therapy work is not for every dog, and one cannot just pick up a dog and take him

Ask the Expert

SHOW DOG OR PET DOG

Q: What is the difference between a pet dog and a show dog? Why do some dogs cost more than others?

A: I hear it all the time: I'm just looking for a pet, not a show dog. While the statement can raise my hackles a little, I understand that most non–dog fancy folks don't understand, and I am glad to give my perspective: There is no difference at all! At least not at my house nor at the homes of most breeders whom I know and work with.

The definition of "pet" as provided by Dictionary.com is as follows: any domesticated or tamed animal that is kept as a companion and cared for affectionately, showing fondness or affection; a thing particularly cherished. And adding my own words: "who may or may not be shown in the show ring." All of my dogs are pets. I could not possibly show them to their fullest potential if it were not for the bond that is so important between a dog and a handler (whether professional or owner/handler), and that is found only in the trusted relationship built with a pet who is shown affection, cherished, and cared for with loving kindness.

So why bother showing? The show ring is where I test my breeding program to see how close I am to the Havanese breed standard. It also tells me if I am producing the healthiest dogs I can because of the testing required or recommended. But not every dog has the conformation or composure to be a show dog. There is no way my Gemma or Bella Rosa were going to stand for going into the show ring, yet they have both produced wonderful champions— as well as cherished pets who have gone to loving homes. Another issue is that showing your dog can be a time-consuming effort, and many families have other priorities, which is just fine. Why shouldn't they have the best pet I can provide? Many of my pups are show-potential pups living quality lives in someone's home, and I'm pleased with that.

I charge one price for a pup, regardless of gender, color, and designation (pet/show), although I'm aware that other breeders price differently. Why do I do this? I don't really think that a show-prospect puppy can be identified until he is 6 months old. Now, if I say he has show potential that means that I've given it my best shot based on history, breeding, whelping, etc., and the pup can be grown out with the goal of showing. However, I do have different contracts for pet and show puppies. A show contract has far more stipulations and obligations, which is pretty straightforward.

If you have specific questions or concerns, most breeders would be more than happy to help you select the best dog for your family and lifestyle because they want their dogs to go to the best homes possible.

—Nancy K. Boyle, Heybern Showdogs; Exhibitor, Breeder, Trainer.

into a nursing home or hospital. Most therapy certification agencies, such as Therapy Dog International and the Delta Society, require a dog to pass the Canine Good Citizenship (CGC) test, which is sponsored by the AKC. And most will not grant certification until the dog is at least 1 year old. You can get more information by visiting these websites: www. therapydogs.com and www.deltasociety. org.

Traveling With Your Havanese

If you enjoy traveling, Havanese can make wonderful companions. But as you would do for yourself, be sure to prepare your dog for travel ahead of time. First, make sure he is healthy and able to accompany you on the road or in the air. Have him checked out by your vet and make sure that you have the necessary medical documents if you are traveling abroad or to a destination that requires vaccination

Havanese make wonderful travel companions, but make sure your pets are healthy and able to comfortably accompany you to your destination.

A doggy travel kit should include everything your Havanese will need while he is away from home.

or two, and a few first-aid items. Be sure to include a collar and leash, and your dog's identifying information, including his microchip number.

Travel by Car

There is an assumption that, because Havanese are toy dogs, they won't encounter the same issues that larger dogs do when traveling. But car travel can and does pose safety concerns and logistical problems for all dogs and their owners.

When traveling by car, your Havanese will need to be confined in a well-secured kennel or crate while the car is in motion, both for his safety and yours. I prefer to travel with my Havanese in a covered crate. If children are along, the crate can be situated in the middle of the back seat so they can play with and distract the dog. Give your dog a toy and a few chews to keep him occupied. When not in the car, a leash is needed to safely walk him at rest areas along the way and during his visit to your destination. Be sure to stop at least every 4 to 5 hours to allow your dog to potty and stretch his legs. During every rest stop, walk him briskly for a few minutes so he can stretch his legs and work off some stress from the trip.

Most importantly, never leave your dog unattended in a parked vehicle. In addition to the possibility of being taken, a dog can suffer heatstroke in a matter of minutes.

records or the like. Also make sure that your destination accepts pets. You don't want to arrive to find that you can't stay there with your pet.

When all arrangements are made, gather everything your dog will need when he is away from home. A doggy travel kit doesn't have to be fancy. It should contain a couple of rolled-up plastic bags to dispose of waste, as well as a roll of paper towels and some wipes, bottled water, some food and treats, bowls, a favorite toy

SWIMMING SAFETY TIPS

Water sports are among the most popular for Havanese. Whether in a kiddies' pool, a boat, or a pond, Havanese seem to love the water. However, that doesn't mean that all Havanese can swim or that they should simply be thrown into water. A Havanese puppy should be introduced to water in stages, just as a young child is introduced to swimming. Here are some important safety tips:

- Its long coat presents a swimming hazard for the breed. A small puppy in full coat can carry the equivalent of up to 2 pounds (1 kg) in hair, enough to drag him down or keep him from swimming to safety. So if water sports play an important part in your summer activities, it's best to keep your Havanese in a puppy cut of about 2 inches (5 cm).
- Teach your dog to swim to the safe end of the pool, where he can easily get out.
- If out boating, be sure that your Havanese wears a doggy life vest. However, first watch him swim with the vest on in shallow water so that you know whether his head is up or forced down because of the vest. You may need to try several styles to find one that is safe for your dog.
- Nets and covers on pools are not useful unless they can support your dog's weight. The best security is a set of eyes always on your dog. Also watch children when playing with dogs around water because they may not always be aware of canine safety issues.

For other excellent tips on summertime water sports for your Havanese, go to: www.petmd.com/blogs/fullyvetted/2007/june/swimming-pool-safety-sweet-summertime.

Travel by Air

Do you dream of your Havanese becoming a frequent flyer, accompanying you on your domestic and international travels? By and large, Havanese travel quite well in airplanes.

There are a few things you can do to help your dog travel more comfortably.

Depending on the duration of the trip, you may need to adjust his feeding schedule; it's best not to feed him the morning of your flight, but you can give him a bit of extra food during dinner the night before. It's also a good idea to fill a small bag with kibble and attach it securely to the kennel in case the plane is grounded and the dog

Many vacation areas now cater to people traveling with their pets. Always call ahead of time to make sure your hotel or resort is pet-friendly.

shipping an animal in cargo, it helps for the staff to know that your dog is traveling with you so that the baggage staffers can remove him from the plane if an emergency should occur. Of course, you may not want to put your dog in cargo, but cabin guidelines sometimes permit only two dogs to travel in the cabin at a time. The best way to fly in cargo is on a direct flight with no stopovers. If it's necessary to send your dog on a flight with stopovers, ask if the airline has an climate-controlled facility and climate-controlled vans that will fetch your dog from the arriving airline and load him onto the connecting flight for the next leg of the trip. Check also to see what weather embargoes the airline has in place. Most airlines will not fly animals in cargo if the temperature is 85°F (29°C) or above.

Pet-Friendly Destinations

Pet policies at most parks, campgrounds, hotels, and motels range from none at all to outright refusal. Some hotels and motels charge a modest deposit for pets to stay overnight. When making reservations, ask for a room on the ground floor, with a door that opens to the outside, preferably situated at the

requires feeding. Allow your dog to have a walk before your flight because he will be confined for quite a while. Take him for one more walk in the airport prior to boarding. Do the same upon arrival at your destination airport.

Pets can travel in two ways on airlines: in an airline-approved soft carry-on bag that will fit under the seat in front of you or in the cargo hold of the plane. While there is paperwork galore involved in

SAFE TRAVEL CHECKLIST

Before you take your Havanese on a trip by air, adhere to the following guidelines:

✓ Vet check your dog to be sure that he is healthy enough for travel.
✓ Obtain documents to verify that he is up to date on immunizations.
✓ Ask the vet to fill out an airline health certificate that affirms your dog is in good health and properly vaccinated.
✓ Make reservations for yourself and your dog as early as possible.
✓ Visit the airline's website to see what its rules are about pets in cabin and cargo.
✓ If traveling in cabin, pet carriers must meet the airline's policies. If in cargo, the crate must meet airline specifications.
✓ Don't medicate your Havanese. Almost every airline will refuse to take a dog who has had some kind of medication such as tranquilizers or antihistamines.
✓ Microchip your pet.
✓ Put together a doggy travel kit to take with you.

rear of the building. In this way, you can take your dog out to potty where there are fewer guests, and if he starts barking, there will be fewer people to hear it. Be a good doggy guest and clean up after your Havanese. Always dispose of waste in a clean and acceptable manner. Putting a blanket over the bedspread to control loose hair is a welcome courtesy gesture. While a Havanese does not shed as badly as some other dogs do, all dogs do blow hair of some kind and it takes a lot to remove it. Remember that your dog's conduct may help determine whether pets will continue to be welcome guests wherever you stay.

Chapter
9

Health of Your Havanese

Just as with ourselves, a healthy lifestyle will promote the overall well-being and longevity of your Havanese. Along with optimal nutrition, regular exercise, and grooming to maintain a healthy coat and skin, your dog needs a veterinary checkup on an annual basis and, of course, as needed throughout his life. And, as a valued member of your family, it is your responsibility to make sure that your dog receives proper preventive care.

Finding a Vet

You've done your homework and you've chosen your new puppy. When you pick him up from the breeder, your contract might well ask that you have a vet examine him within three to five working days, even if the puppy was vet checked shortly before coming to you. If you know for sure which puppy you are getting out of a litter, then you have some time to shop around to locate a veterinarian and to make an appointment.

How do you know that you are making the best choice for you and your pet's needs? You must educate yourself about your new puppy and any issues specific to the breed. Don't be surprised if the vet you choose has never seen a Havanese before. They are still rare enough that not all vet practices have one as a client.

Here are some tips on how to find the perfect vet practice for you and your dog:

- First, if you know someone who has a Havanese, ask which vet she uses, why she uses her, and if she is happy with their relationship.
- Schedule an introductory visit with the vet, but be considerate of her time because this is to be a brief visit. As you enter, notice how odor-free the office is and how environmentally clean and organized it is. Ask if you can take a tour of non-public spaces in the practice.
- The front office staff is usually the first line of defense for the veterinarian, so their demeanor and skills in managing a veterinary practice should be important to you. Are they empathetic and compassionate, and do they handle their pet clients with care and respect? Are they polite and courteous, and willing to listen to whatever information you bring in? Are they interested in how much information you have about your pet, and do they seem committed to helping you become an educated client?
- Before you leave, discuss veterinary fees. I've found that requesting an estimate of fees for a visit is well received. Have a frank discussion with your vet about the services provided and those that may not be provided. How flexible is the practice concerning developing a plan of care when there are medical and/or financial restraints? Explore with your veterinarian those

Annual veterinary checkups are essential if you want your dog to stay healthy.

things you can do or learn to do to keep costs in line. Ask if your vet accepts pet insurance and which policies she would recommend. This can also help keep costs down.

The Annual Vet Visit

Your first vet visit will be the wellness visit your pup receives after you bring him home. Chances are he still needs to complete his series of "puppy shots" as well as to be checked for parasites and overall good health. But your pet should also continue to have an annual vet visit to update vaccines and check his general health, especially during his first 7 years, which is the most rapid growth period for your Havanese. Before your annual visit, however, you should be prepared.

- Bring your pet into the vet's office either in a small crate if appropriate (my preference) or at least on a collar and leash. He may become nervous and excited by the experience, and this will help to keep him out of trouble. Also, you may be able to prevent him from being too close to other animals who may be contagious.
- Obtain and bring a stool sample.
- Bring your dog's health care

information with you if you are switching veterinarians, including his vaccination record.

- Make a list of questions you might have.
- If you have pet insurance, bring your insurance card.

During a general exam, a vet tech or veterinary nurse will weigh your dog and record his temperature and pulse. The veterinarian then follows with a physical exam, going over different parts of your dog's body. She will examine his eyes, nose, ears, and mouth looking for any signs of a problem. Next the chest and abdomen are examined. The vet listens to the lungs and heart. She palpates the abdomen to check for internal problems, and then examines the bone structure. The skin and coat will also be checked. After this, preparations are made to give any necessary vaccines.

Vaccinations

Clearly, the development of canine vaccines has enabled our pets to live longer, healthier lives. But second only to the controversies surrounding canine nutrition are the controversies surrounding canine vaccinations. Many breeders and some vets feel that pets are being overvaccinated. The position of the American Animal Hospital Association (AAHA) is that decisions regarding vaccination protocols are best left up to the local clinician or veterinarian, although monitoring these controversies remains a part of the AAHA's research program.

At the forefront of studies about immunization schedules and their effects has been Dr. W. Jean Dodds, director of Hemopet. Broadly speaking, Dr. Dodds' studies have been concerned with the problem of overvaccination, which may result in *vaccinosis*, as well as an assortment of autoimmune disorders. Vaccinosis occurs as a reaction to being vaccinated or overvaccinated. Clinical symptoms of reactions to a vaccine include fever, stiffness, sore joints, abdominal tenderness, susceptibility to infections, neurological disorders, and encephalitis.

There is some question about the Havanese being a "vaccine-sensitive" breed. In light of what seems to be a problem of overvaccination, many Havanese breeders have adopted Dr. Dodds' vaccination protocol, which also includes using vaccine titers to evaluate the need for annual vaccinations. Vaccine titers are blood tests that measure whether or not an animal currently has protection against a certain disease. Additionally, some breeders have chosen to not "bundle" shots, separating out the puppy shots from the rabies inoculation in an effort to prevent adverse vaccination reactions. The decision of which vaccines to give is also affected by the environment in which we live. For example, during a visit to my vet, as we were discussing what we were going to do with my new puppies, and she pointed out that because we live in a heavily forested area with many deer, one would think that Lyme disease (obtained from the brown tick) would be rampant. Not so, according to their records. They only treat five to ten cases of Lyme disease per year. However, they diagnose four to five cases of heartworms a week despite the spraying associated with an agricultural area. So where you live and the conditions under which you live will have an impact on you and your vet's decisions about vaccinations. Include questions about vaccination schedules and requirements in your conversation with your vet at your first wellness visit. Havanese remain rare enough that most vets have not yet met the breed and thus have limited experience with it.

The following is a copy of Dr. Dodds' latest revision to the vaccination schedule. Please copy it and take it with you to your vet. Having attended many of Dr. Jean Dodds' lectures and read her work widely, I feel comfortable providing her latest canine vaccination protocol.

CANINE VACCINATION PROTOCOL 2009—MINIMAL VACCINE USE

by W. Jean Dodds, DVM, HEMOPET

The following vaccine protocol is offered for those dogs where minimal vaccinations are advisable or desirable. The schedule is one I recommend and should not be interpreted to mean that other protocols recommended by a veterinarian would be less satisfactory. It's a matter of professional judgment and choice.

Age of Puppy	Vaccine Type
9 –10 weeks	Distemper + Parvovirus, MLV (modified live virus)
14 weeks	Same as above
16 –18 weeks (optional)	Same as above
20 weeks or older, if allowable by law	Rabies
1 year	Distemper + Parvovirus, MLV (modified live virus)
1 year	Rabies, killed 3-year produce (give 3–4 weeks apart from distemper/parvovirus booster)

Perform vaccine antibody titers for distemper and parvovirus annually thereafter. Vaccinate for rabies virus according to the law, except where circumstances indicate that a written waiver needs to be obtained from the primary care veterinarian. In that case, a rabies antibody titer can also be performed to accompany the waiver request.

W. Jean Dodds, DVM

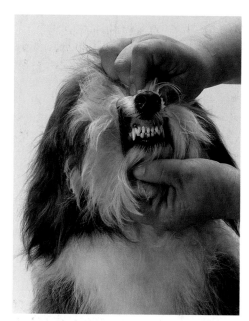

During an annual checkup, your dog will get a complete physical examination and receive updates on necessary vaccinations or medications.

Diseases Commonly Vaccinated Against

There are two categories of vaccination: core vaccines and noncore vaccines. Core vaccines are those that all dogs should have, such as distemper, parvovirus, canine adenovirus-2, and rabies. The second category is noncore vaccines, and these are recommended for dogs who have an increased risk of exposure to certain diseases, such as Lyme disease and leptospirosis. As discussed, determine your dog's vaccination protocol with your vet.

Bordetella (Noncore)

Bordetella is a highly contagious bacterial disease. It is also called kennel cough or canine whooping cough. Symptoms range from mild to severe and include a dry cough, sneezing, anorexia, fever, coughing up blood, and malaise. If it is a mild case, the disease may clear up on its own but will take about 3 weeks to do so. More severe cases will require antibiotic treatment to suppress the chance of a secondary infection.

Whether to give the bordetella vaccine depends on your lifestyle. Be aware, though, that most grooming shops and commercial dog boarding establishments require the bordetella vaccine be given in advance of the dog's stay.

Canine Adenovirus-2 (Core)

Like the bordetella vaccine, the canine adenovirus vaccine protects against various strains of upper respiratory illnesses, but it is given primarily to protect against hepatitis. Respiratory symptoms include sneezing, chest congestion, fever, and cough. Liver-related symptoms include abdominal tenderness, jaundice, and increased thirst and urination. Treatment consists of IV fluids and supportive treatment. There are no known side effects to the vaccine.

Distemper (Core)

Distemper is a highly contagious virus that

resembles the measles virus. It is spread in aerosol droplets released through coughing and sneezing, feces, and urine. The virus first appears in the respiratory tract and then replicates in lymphatic tissue, allowing it to invade the abdominal cavity. The illness lasts about 3 weeks if the dog lives that long. The ability to survive depends upon the strength and maturity of the dog's immune system. Until recently, supportive care was the limit of care available. In the past 4 years, however, researchers have found a positive response of the infection to high doses of vitamin A and ribavirin.

Leptospirosis (Noncore)

Leptospirosis is a bacterial infection that affects the liver and kidneys. Leptospira are found most often in warm, wet environments. So if you live in the northern part of the United States, your pet would be less likely to contract it. Although no two cases progress in the same way, they do have common symptoms of fever, dehydration, chills, shivering, and stiffness. Leptospirosis is a zoonotic disease, meaning it can be transferred between animals and humans. The mode of transmission is usually through dog or rat urine. Therefore, strict sanitary measures can forestall it. Medical treatment includes broad-spectrum antibiotics. Intense supportive care is essential in the early stages, such as emetics for vomiting and intravenous fluids for rehydration.

Parainfluenza (Noncore)

Like bordetella and canine adenovirus, parainfluenza is another highly contagious respiratory disease. The parainfluenza vaccine is one of the vaccines included in "puppy shots."

Bacterial diseases are often spread through direct contact, so vaccination is sometimes advised for dogs who will be regularly exposed to other canines at doggy day care, dog parks, or during shows and other events.

Symptoms include runny nose, malaise, and labored breathing, which becomes increasingly acute with activity. Because it is so contagious, the disease should be contained as quickly as possible. Your vet will begin antibacterial and antiviral therapies, and your dog should be kept in a crate/room where there is as little stress as possible, with a humidifier to ease his respiration.

Parvovirus (Core)

Nothing gives me the chills more than hearing a diagnosis of parvovirus. This serious viral disease affects puppies more than adults. Intestinal symptoms include diarrhea that is usually bloody and emits a foul smell, lethargy, vomiting, loss of appetite, and in severe cases, a raw intestinal tract that twists to create a blockage. While there is treatment for it, puppies rarely survive. Vaccination against it remains the first line of defense.

Rabies (Core)

Rabies is one of the most deadly of neurological viral diseases, and it can be passed from animals to humans, so this vaccine is mandated by law. Although there is some controversy about not doing rabies titers before updating vaccinations, the issue of vaccinosis (side effects) is much less a danger than contracting the disease. Rabies travels along the peripheral nerves into the brain, causing encephalitis. Early symptoms include malaise, anxiety, and hydrophobia (fear of water). Symptoms later progress into partial or complete paralysis. It is only a matter of days until the dog dies.

Spaying and Neutering

Spaying is abdominal surgery in a female dog (hystero-oophorectomy) to remove her ovaries and uterus. Neutering is castration, or the surgical removal of both testicles of a male dog. Likely your breeder will insert a neuter (for males) and spay (for females) clause in the purchase contract requiring your puppy to be sterilized. Like vaccinations, spaying and neutering has become a controversial issue. The controversy centers around several issues: the age at which sterilization is performed, health consequences, and personality changes.

The primary reason to spay or neuter your Havanese is to prevent her or him from breeding. Unless you are certain you want to show and breed your dog, this procedure is the humane and responsible option. On any given day, 60 percent of unwanted dogs in animal shelters are killed. So the primary reason to sterilize has been to help cut back on the overpopulation of abandoned animals.

There is less agreement on what age to have this surgery done. Sex hormones affect bone structure, so if you want your Havanese to be more on the body builder

If you are not a professional Havanese breeder, have your dog neutered or spayed.

side, wait a bit to neuter him. Similarly, if you want your female Havanese to retain her girlie features, then wait a bit. Rarely do I neuter/spay at 6 months any longer. The range for our spay/neuter procedure is 9 to 12 months.

Health consequences consist of positive and negative benefits, depending upon the age of the dog when he or she has the surgery. On the negative side, if it's done before 1 year of age, spaying and neutering can increase the incidence of orthopedic disorders. However, sterilization does help prevent the development of perianal fistulas and osteosarcoma. The benefit to females is that they pretty much escape malignant mammary tumors, as well as a deadly uterine disease called pyometria. In most cases of pyometria, a hysterectomy will be necessary. The benefit to males is the lowering of prostate cancer and less territorial marking.

Personality change is a myth that just won't go away. Whatever personality quirks and features your dog had before the surgery will be there after the surgery. Both types of surgeries are safe, and the recovery time swift. So do consider spaying or neutering your Havanese.

Parasites

What to do? Your sweet puppy is running around, licking his own and everyone else's behind, drinking and tasting everything, and you seem to be winning the battle of the clean house. Yet his fecal exam at the vet still shows that he has worms! First, these are all activities that puppies engage in, and the presence and/or absence of parasites has little to do with them. Grown dogs carry parasites and are, for the most part, able to shake it off, but puppies are not so fortunate—and for them, some parasites can be deadly. The following are some of the most common internal and external parasites.

Internal Parasites

The symptoms of intestinal worms are usually visible, causing your puppy to drag his bottom across the floor, lick his anus incessantly, and if not corrected right away, exhibit a bloated abdomen. However, the best way to determine if your puppy has worms is via a fecal exam by your veterinarian. When puppy first arrives at your house, work with your vet to set up a regular deworming schedule that suits the geography of the area in which you live.

Heartworms

Heartworms (*Dirofilaria immitis*) are roundworm parasites that live in the lungs and blood vessels and are transmitted through mosquito bites. Symptoms include labored breathing with little exercise, fainting, vomiting, and, in the end stages, congestive heart failure. The best treatment is a monthly preventive containing ivermectin. The treatment for existing heartworms takes several weeks and intensely stresses an already stressed dog.

Hookworms

Hookworms are nematodes that live in a dog's intestines. They attach to the bowel and suck blood, eventually causing anemia. Hookworms are transmitted through mother's milk, and the disease is especially fatal in puppies. Although some puppies show no symptoms, others may not look well. Later stages may include symptoms such as bloody diarrhea, anemia, and weight loss. Treatment includes an antiworm medication and usually nutritional supplements if your puppy becomes anemic.

Roundworms

Roundworms (*Toxascaris canis, T. leonina*) exist in more than 1,000 varieties. Roundworms are among the most common parasites affecting dogs. Distribution occurs through feces; fresh feces are not contagious, but older feces are. *Toxascaris* are passed thru the mother via grooming, soil, and the natural tendency of the parasite to infest organs such as mammary glands and the uterus from whence they enter the intestinal tract. It is important to realize that the deworming treatments available do not

NONTOXIC PARASITE CONTROL

Q: I want to protect my Havanese from parasites, but I don't really like the thought of using chemicals on my lawn or in my house. Is there some other alternative I can use that is less toxic?

A: If you don't have a flea problem but worry about flea infestation, you can try some easy-to-use natural alternatives. If fleas have already gained entry to your home on your Havanese, there are also many nontoxic ways to address an infestation. You may not think that you have an infestation if you only find a few fleas on your Havanese, but remember that for every flea hanging out on your dog, there may be many more in his environment. But before reaching for chemicals, poisons, or pesticides, try these safer, more natural options:

- Add brewer's yeast, garlic, or apple cider vinegar to your dog's food.
- Add five drops of grapefruit seed extract to your dog's water each time you fill up his bowl. It not only helps to prevent fleas and ticks from taking up residence on your dog by changing his immune response, but it also helps prevent and protect him from other parasites like Giardia, coccidia, and general tummy troubles from any bacteria in his food or something he shouldn't have eaten.
- Citrus is a natural flea deterrent. Pour a cup of boiling water over a sliced lemon. Include the lemon skin, scored to release more citrus oil. Let this mixture soak overnight and sponge or spray it on your dog to kill fleas instantly. The spray also works *great* as a preventive—carry it with you and spray some liberally on his legs and tummy before visiting grassy areas. You can also save any leftover portions in the fridge for up to seven days.
- Bathe and comb your dog regularly. Use mild soap, not insecticides. If fleas are found on the comb, dip the comb in a glass of soapy water. Ivory soap has an excellent reputation for safely and gently killing fleas if you find any. Use Ivory soap full strength and let the lather sit on him for three to five minutes (longer if you found a lot of fleas). The soap will kill them. Then rinse him off and bathe him with a good-quality dog shampoo and conditioner.
- Cedar shampoo, cedar oil, and cedar-filled sleeping mats are commercially available. Cedar repels many insects, including fleas. Try a web search for pet-safe cedar products. My Havanese have homemade, unstained cedar boxes for beds. You can buy cedar wood at big box hardware stores.

—Robin Moser, Havana Silk Dogs Havanese; Exhibitor, Breeder, Author.

Always check your dog for fleas, ticks, and mites if he's been playing outdoors.

Tapeworms

Tapeworms require an intermediary host to infect your dog, the most common being fleas. The dog ingests a flea that contains tapeworm larvae, which then hatch in the intestinal tract and attach to the intestinal lining to feed. Visible symptoms are rare but may include diarrhea and soft stools. Diagnosing tapeworms requires that your vet perform a fecal test to check for them. The most consistent level of treatment needed is to eliminate fleas, combined with a deworming program using prescription medication. Most over-the-counter products to deworm for tapeworm are ineffective.

External Parasites

External parasites, such as fleas, mites, and ticks, can also present problems for your dog, causing him great discomfort. Using only one approach to eliminate external parasites is likely to be ineffective. For example, along with flea and tick preventives, bedding will need to be washed regularly and food dishes sterilized by using the dishwasher set on its highest temperature.

kill the parasite. Rather they anesthetize the parasites so that they release their hold and are either coughed up or evacuated in stool. Although you might possibly see some worms still living when they are evacuated, they cannot live in the outside environment.

A plethora of flea and tick preventive products are available, so discuss which ones may be the best option for your Havanese with your vet.

Fleas

Fleas are insects that live by feeding on the blood of mammals, including humans. Your first clue that fleas are present will likely occur before you even see a flea: Your Havanese will be scratching constantly!

To check for these pesky parasites, examine your pet thoroughly, paying special attention to the neck, underbelly, and base of the tail. Additionally, using a flea comb that will get deeper into your dog's coat will allow you to be more positive about whether or not you have a flea infestation.

While you are washing bedding, wash your pet in either an antiflea dog shampoo or just a gentle dog shampoo. When finished, put a fresh new flea collar on him and then address the infestation, which is sure to be in your house. Inspect your house for fleas, vacuum thoroughly, and then use whatever household preventive products you feel necessary. Don't forget to spray your yard, too, which is likely where your dog picked up those fleas.

Mites

Mites are members of the arachnid, or spider, family and comprise many different varieties. Ear mites (*Otodectes cynotis*) are the most common type affecting dogs. Although they can exist on the skin on any part of the body, they become most evident in the ears. You'll see your dog scratching or shaking his head in an effort to dislodge something that is small and barely visible to the naked eye. Mites will not go away unless treatment includes an insecticide such as pyrethrin, a contact poison. Pyrethrin-containing products are available over the counter as well as prescribed by your veterinarian. If you suspect your pet has mites, take him to the vet to be checked.

To prevent ear mites, begin getting your puppy accustomed to having his ears handled and cleaned regularly. Cleaning his ears can be done with any high-end ear cleaner. I like those cleaners that contain Malaseb best because this ingredient helps the ear dry out faster after it is cleaned. For more on how to clean your dog's ears, see Chapter 5.

Ticks

Ticks, like mites, are members of the arachnid family. Their bite is generally painless and not noticed until the tick falls off. Bite sizes can range from barely visible to as large as pea. Although most tick bites are innocuous, sometimes dangerous pathogens are secreted in the bite, causing infectious illness such as Lyme disease.

Removing a tick has three goals: prevent the spread of pathogens, get out all of the tick, and provide medical treatment if needed. To safely remove the tick, gloves, tweezers, and a protected area should be used. Use tweezers to grasp the back of the tick's head and pull the tick straight out; rocking it back and forth only stimulates the production of toxins. Do not squash the tick once it is out; rather flush it down the drain or commode.

Symptoms of tick-borne diseases can include fever, lethargy, and muscle weakness. If you see symptoms and suspect infection, take your dog to his vet. If your dog tests positive, medication will be prescribed.

Breed-Specific Illnesses

Like other breeds, Havanese unfortunately have the potential to develop some fairly significant breed-specific health issues. Some of these conditions can be inherited, and most can be detected through testing.

The Havanese Club of America (HCA) has taken the lead for more than 10 years in educating breeders and pet owners alike about the health and care of the Havanese. Many breeders go beyond the recommended testing in their efforts to improve the breed, and the Havanese fancy has been extremely dedicated to producing as healthy a dog as possible and increasing the transparency required in such efforts.

While Havanese are generally a healthy breed, it's important to educate yourself about those conditions that may affect your dog. Your breeder and veterinarian can answer any questions you may have regarding these concerns.

Cataracts

Cataracts occur when lens fibers in the eye break down, causing reduced transparency of the lens (opacity) and, eventually, vision impairment. This can occur at any age. Causes can be hereditary or the result of trauma. Once the deterioration of the lens has begun, the only correction is cataract surgery.

As noted in Chapter 1, the HCA has been engaged in a long and sustained campaign to test for cataracts at 1 year of age and to the file the results with the Canine Education Research Foundation (CERF). As of 2006, 92 percent of tests done on the Havanese have been reported normal.

Cherry Eye

Cherry eye (canine nictitans gland prolapses) occurs when the third eyelid prolapses, or "hangs out." While not fatal or serious, it can become a problem if not taken care of immediately. The third eyelid is responsible for providing tears to moisten your dog's eyes. Drying out of the eye can result in additional trauma and infection. Surgery is the treatment of choice.

PUPPY FIRST AID

Although we do our best to keep our dogs safe, there are times when disaster strikes. Puppies are curious and explore everything, and they can sometimes find themselves in hazardous situations in a matter of seconds. Besides puppy-proofing your home and yard and keeping a first-aid kit at the ready, learn what to do in an emergency.

Two of the most frequent and deadly categories of puppy accidents are choking and poisoning. Here's what you need to know:

Choking

The causes of choking may be internal (health-related) or external (caused by something in the environment). For example, puppies are still young and might not know how to thoroughly expectorate after coughing. Monitor your puppy if he is ill or coughing to prevent possible choking problems. An external reason may be that your puppy has a small object lodged in his throat, such as a piece of a toy, treat, bone, etc. Never feed your puppy cooked bones or treats that are too small. Pick up any toys and objects, such as string, buttons, and the like, that could be dangerous if swallowed. Always supervise your dog when he is given treats or toys.

If you suspect your puppy is choking, lay him gently on your lap, with his stomach against your knee. Then, place your hands on his back and push up gently against it. Be firm but careful not to be too rough or you may injure his back or ribs. Repeat this several times if necessary. If the object does not dislodge, take your puppy to the vet immediately.

Poisoning

You may not see signs and symptoms of poisoning until several hours after ingestion of the toxic substance. These signs include excessive vomiting, excessive salivating, abdominal pain, constipation, diarrhea, dehydration, stumbling or muscular weakness, respiratory problems, partial paralysis, and unconsciousness.

If you suspect that your puppy may have ingested something toxic, call your vet immediately for advice. Tell her what your dog ingested (if you know) and describe any symptoms you recognize. Or, if it's after hours, call the ASPCA's Animal Poison Control Center at 1-888-426-4435. The hotline is always open and manned by certified veterinarians. For extreme cases of poisoning, get your dog to an emergency clinic immediately.

Common pet toxins, as reported by the ASPCA, include human and veterinary medications; people foods, especially chocolate, onions, and garlic; household cleaners; insecticides and rodenticides; solvents and antifreeze; and certain indoor and outdoor plants. Visit their website at www.aspca.org for more information.

Knowing how to recognize potential health problems and how to handle them is important to your dog's overall well-being.

Chondrodysplasia

Chondrodysplasia is a genetic orthopedic disorder identified by short legs and bowed front legs. It may be accompanied by other illnesses such as congestive heart and kidney failure. A Havanese with chondrodysplasia can live a fulfilled family life and not suffer any more problems. However, it is recommended that dogs with this disorder not be included in breeding programs.

Congenital Deafness

Canine congenital deafness is considered hereditary and is linked to color patterns. While the Havanese show only 0.1 percent of deafness in those dogs tested, it wasn't until breeders learned of the disorder through testing that they were able to make better-informed decisions about their breeding programs. Unfortunately, there is no cure for canine congenital deafness, and dogs so afflicted should be removed from breeding programs.

Hip Dysplasia

Another test done for structural soundness is the test for hip dysplasia, a disorder most often found in larger breeds. It refers to laxity or looseness in the hips, which may start when the dog is immature and advance with development. Hip dysplasia might be suspected when your dog is seen walking like someone with arthritis. Depending on the severity of the dysplasia, a number of surgical approaches may be chosen. Nonsurgical approaches include weight management, warmth, a supportive sleeping area, and oral supplements.

The Orthopedic Foundation for Animals (OFA) reports that in those Havanese born between 2001 and 2005, only 2.4 percent of the 251 Havanese tested were dysplastic. Although the OFA will do a preliminary hip exam, it does not issue a certification until the dog reaches 2 years of age because bone plates are still shifting and changing until then.

Legg-Calve-Perthes Disease (LCPD)

LCPD is found in humans and dogs, but is not zoonotic. Also known as avascular necrosis of the femoral head, symptoms appear between the ages of 4 months and 1 year. Clinical symptoms are primarily limping and refusing to go up and down stairs. The only corrective is surgery and pain medicine when needed.

Liver Shunt

Also known as portosystemic shunt (PSS), this is a condition in which a blood vessel bypasses the liver before the blood has a chance to be filtered. PSS can be congenital or acquired after birth. The puppy fails to grow at a normal rate, vacillating between gaining too much weight and not gaining enough weight. Vomiting, diarrhea, and behavioral changes, such as staring off into space, will also be present. In the past 5 years, great strides have been made in the treatment of PSS. Treatment now takes a multifaceted approach that includes nutritional supplements, medication, and surgery.

Patellar Luxation

The patella, or kneecap, is situated in a groove that allows it to slide up and down. If the groove is too shallow, then the kneecap "jumps" out of position when the leg is extended backward. Luxating patellas are graded 1 to 4 in level of severity, with grade 1 being the mildest disease and grade 4 being the worst. A luxating patella or "trick knee" is diagnosed by palpation and x-ray. Symptoms range from mild intermittent limping on rear legs to the dog walking on its front legs because the rear legs are so painful. Surgery remains the treatment of choice.

General Illnesses

General illnesses are those that occur across the dog population and are not necessarily breed specific. Some of these can be prevented and/or treated with routine care at home, and others require veterinary care. In any case, regardless of what the health issues are, always seek veterinary advice if you have any concerns.

Allergies

Allergies are somewhat common culprits of general illness in dogs. It is ironic to think that a breed that is supposed to be hypoallergenic toward humans might itself be allergic to grass, food, cleaners, and the like. However, dogs react differently to allergies than people do. Most often, they tend to scratch, lick, or chew on their irritated skin to alleviate itching and discomfort. Some may have red, inflamed skin, especially on the belly, if they have a contact allergy to environmental allergens such as pollens or garden and household chemicals. Food allergies can cause similar symptoms. Although fairly rare in Havanese, there have been some instances of suspected food allergies. A food allergy might disturb his eating and evacuation habits. If it is severe enough, your dog might whine due to abdominal pain. Your veterinarian may prescribe antibiotics and steroids depending on the severity.

Cancer

Surprisingly, cancer is the leading cause of death in all breeds, but advances have been made in canine cancer detection and treatment. One of the strongest arguments for spaying a female dog is to prevent the development of mammary cancers. These are usually first evidenced by lumps along the nipple lines. Bladder and prostate cancer seem to occur more frequently in males who have not been neutered, so altering has its advantages here as well. Your dog might have difficulty urinating or might urinate blood if he has these cancers. Treatment varies with the type of cancer and includes nonmedical as well as surgical treatments.

Alternative Therapies

Until recently, it was thought that alternative therapies were for desperate pet owners whose animals had not responded to conventional medicine. However, there's much more to it than the use of herbs and roots. Today, complementary treatments integrate alternative canine therapies and traditional veterinary medicine. Referred to as complementary and alternative medicine (CAM), this methodology proposes that each alternative/complementary approach can bring something to the table to improve the health of your dog.

Acupuncture may be used as an alternative to traditional medicine to prevent disease and provide support to the immune system by stimulating the body's healing and pain-relieving mechanisms.

Acupuncture

Used to strengthen weakened immune systems, acupuncture is just one of several forms of traditional Chinese medicine (TCM). Using some of the 365 acupoints on the body, the practitioner inserts long metal needles into specific areas relative to the dog's condition. This process releases endorphins, hormones, and other healing and pain-relieving mechanisms, which stimulates the healing process Expect your dog to have at least three to six treatments, combined with nutritional supplements, lifestyle changes, and adherence to any medicine regimen ordered.

Chiropractic

Canine chiropractic is used to treat, among other disorders, event or sports-related injuries, muscle and back pain, as well as bladder, bowel, and other internal disorders. Therapy consists of manipulation of the spine and joints to

Herbal remedies can be used to treat a variety of canine disorders, but check with your veterinarian before using them.

support healing. However, dogs can suffer side effects from herbal supplements. Do not use herbal remedies without first consulting with your veterinarian.

Homeopathic Medicine

Developed in the 1800s by Dr. Samuel Hahnemann, homeopathy is the practice of treating a disease by using very small doses of a natural substance that would produce the same symptoms of that disease in healthy individuals. It is based on the principle that "like cures like." Some compare it to vaccinations, except that homeopathy uses naturally derived products. Homeopathic remedies use plants, minerals, and other natural substances to stimulate the body's natural defenses and to promote healing. Again, if you are interested in using these remedies, find a homeopathic veterinarian who can guide you.

Massage

Canine massage, similar to human massage, has gained momentum in the last third of the 20th century. It is used for many of the same reasons: it provides relief from muscle pain, aids in rehabilitation of injury, and promotes emotional well-being. It should never be used in lieu of veterinary medical care.

Senior Dog Care

Not only are humans living longer, but so

correct vertebral subluxations, which are areas of the spine that are out of alignment. Chiropractic is often used in conjunction with exercise, massage, acupuncture, and other alternative therapies.

Herbal Remedies

Herbal remedies can be used to treat a variety of canine disorders. The medicinal properties of plants are used as both supplements to help maintain good health and as medicines to treat symptoms and

Check It Out

FINDING A GOOD VET

✓ Find a vet who encourages the relationship among you, your Havanese, and herself, so that you can successfully work together to promote the care and well-being of your dog.
✓ The best care is preventive care, so be sure that your vet gives you a checkup schedule.
✓ Have a frank talk with your vet after reading resource materials about canine vaccination protocols before deciding whether to vaccinate or not.
✓ Review resource materials about parasites so you know what to look for and can prevent them.
✓ Get your pet examined by the vet annually, and have his eyes and patellae check at every visit.
✓ Have a well-stocked first-aid kit in the house, and be familiar with emergency procedures.
✓ Pet-proof your house for safety.

are our dogs. How long they live depends on many factors, not the least of which are good care and lots of love. But breed and size are also related to longevity. The results of a study on dog longevity by Dr. Kelly M. Cassidy, DVM, estimated the average lifespan for the Havanese at 10.25 years.

Our Maddie is 13 years old, and aside from senile cataracts and some deafness, she is fine. In human years, she would be 65 years old. We have some idea of what to expect as we get older, but what can we expect for our beloved Havanese as he gets older? Perhaps the first thing you will

notice is a little graying on his muzzle. He may begin slowing down or taking longer to get up and down stairs, or he may avoid them. He may sleep more and become tired more quickly. Other changes may include decreased vision and hearing. Our responsibility is to make sure that our seniors' needs are met, which are the same as those for any dog: good and age-appropriate nutrition, regular grooming, daily physical and mental stimulation, veterinary care, and lots companionship. Your dog's overall quality of life should be the most important factor to consider as he advances in age.

Resources

Associations and Organizations

Breed Clubs

American Kennel Club (AKC)
5580 Centerview Drive
Raleigh, NC 27606
Telephone: (919) 233-9767
Fax: (919) 233-3627
E-Mail: info@akc.org
www.akc.org

Canadian Kennel Club (CKC)
89 Skyway Avenue, Suite 100
Etobicoke, Ontario M9W 6R4
Telephone: (416) 675-5511
Fax: (416) 675-6506
E-Mail: information@ckc.ca
www.ckc.ca

Federation Cynologique Internationale (FCI)
Secretariat General de la FCI
Place Albert 1er, 13
B – 6530 Thuin
Belgique
www.fci.be

Havanese Club of America (HCA)
www.havanese.org

Havanese Club of Canada (HCC)
www.havanesefanciers.com

The Havanese Club of Great Britain
www.havaneseclub.co.uk

The Kennel Club
1 Clarges Street
London
W1J 8AB
Telephone: 0870 606 6750
Fax: 0207 518 1058
www.the-kennel-club.org.uk

United Kennel Club (UKC)
100 E. Kilgore Road
Kalamazoo, MI 49002-5584
Telephone: (269) 343-9020
Fax: (269) 343-7037
E-Mail: pbickell@ukcdogs.com
www.ukcdogs.com

Pet Sitters

National Association of Professional Pet Sitters
15000 Commerce Parkway, Suite C
Mt. Laurel, NJ 08054
Telephone: (856) 439-0324
Fax: (856) 439-0525
E-Mail: napps@ahint.com
www.petsitters.org

Pet Sitters International
201 East King Street
King, NC 27021-9161
Telephone: (336) 983-9222
Fax: (336) 983-5266
E-Mail: info@petsit.com
www.petsit.com

Rescue Organizations and Animal Welfare Groups

American Humane Association (AHA)
63 Inverness Drive East
Englewood, CO 80112
Telephone: (303) 792-9900
Fax: 792-5333
www.americanhumane.org

American Society for the Prevention of Cruelty to Animals (ASPCA)
424 E. 92nd Street
New York, NY 10128-6804
Telephone: (212) 876-7700
www.aspca.org

The Humane Society of the United States
(HSUS)
2100 L Street, NW
Washington, DC 20037
Telephone: (202) 452-1100
www.hsus.org

Royal Society for the Prevention of Cruelty to
Animals (RSPCA)
RSPCA Enquiries Service
Wilberforce Way, Southwater,
Horsham, West Sussex RH13 9RS
United Kingdom
Telephone: 0870 3335 999
Fax: 0870 7530 284
www.rspca.org.uk

Sports

International Agility Link (IAL)
Global Administrator: Steve Drinkwater
E-Mail: yunde@powerup.au
www.agilityclick.com/~ial

The World Canine Freestyle Organization, Inc.
P.O. Box 350122
Brooklyn, NY 11235
Telephone: (718) 332-8336
Fax: (718) 646-2686
E-Mail: WCFODOGS@aol.com
www.worldcaninefreestyle.org

Therapy

Delta Society
875 124th Ave, NE, Suite 101
Bellevue, WA 98005
Telephone: (425) 679-5500
Fax: (425) 679-5539
E-Mail: info@DeltaSociety.org
www.deltasociety.org

Therapy Dogs Inc.
P.O. Box 20227
Cheyenne, WY 82003
Telephone: (877) 843-7364
Fax: (307) 638-2079
E-Mail: therapydogsinc@qwestoffice.net
www.therapydogs.com

Therapy Dogs International (TDI)
88 Bartley Road
Flanders, NJ 07836
Telephone: (973) 252-9800
Fax: (973) 252-7171
E-Mail: tdi@gti.net
www.tdi-dog.org

Training

Association of Pet Dog Trainers (APDT)
150 Executive Center Drive, Box 35
Greenville, SC 29615
Telephone: (800) PET-DOGS
Fax: (864) 331-0767
E-Mail: information@apdt.com
www.apdt.com

International Association of Animal Behavior
Consultants (IAABC)
565 Callery Road
Cranberry Township, PA 16066
E-Mail: info@iaabc.org
www.iaabc.org

National Association of Dog Obedience
Instructors (NADOI)
PMB 369
729 Grapevine Hwy.
Hurst, TX 76054-2085
www.nadoi.org

Veterinary and Health Resources

Academy of Veterinary Homeopathy (AVH)
P.O. Box 9280
Wilmington, DE 19809
Telephone: (866) 652-1590
Fax: (866) 652-1590
www.theavh.org

American Academy of Veterinary Acupuncture
(AAVA)
P.O. Box 1058
Glastonbury, CT 06033
Telephone: (860) 632-9911
Fax: (860) 659-8772
www.aava.org

American Animal Hospital Association
(AAHA)
12575 W. Bayaud Ave.
Lakewood, CO 80228
Telephone: (303) 986-2800
Fax: (303) 986-1700
E-Mail: info@aahanet.org
www.aahanet.org/index.cfm

American College of Veterinary Internal
Medicine (ACVIM)
1997 Wadsworth Blvd., Suite A
Lakewood, CO 80214-5293
Telephone: (800) 245-9081
Fax: (303) 231-0880
E-Mail: ACVIM@ACVIM.org
www.acvim.org

American College of Veterinary
Ophthalmologists (ACVO)
P.O. Box 1311
Meridian, ID 83860
Telephone: (208) 466-7624
Fax: (208) 466-7693
E-Mail: office09@acvo.com
www.acvo.com

American Holistic Veterinary Medical
Association (AHVMA)
2218 Old Emmorton Road
Bel Air, MD 21015
Telephone: (410) 569-0795
Fax: (410) 569-2346
E-Mail: office@ahvma.org
www.ahvma.org

American Veterinary Medical Association
(AVMA)
1931 North Meacham Road, Suite 100
Schaumburg, IL 60173-4360
Telephone: (847) 925-8070
Fax: (847) 925-1329
E-Mail: avmainfo@avma.org
www.avma.org

ASPCA Animal Poison Control Center
Telephone: (888) 426-4435
www.aspca.org

British Veterinary Association (BVA)
7 Mansfield Street
London
W1G 9NQ
United Kingdom
Telephone: 0207 636 6541
Fax: 0207 908 6349
E-Mail: bvahq@bva.co.uk
www.bva.co.uk

Canine Eye Registration Foundation (CERF)
VMDB/CERF
1717 Philo Rd.
P O Box 3007
Urbana, IL 61803-3007
Telephone: (217) 693-4800
Fax: (217) 693-4801
E-Mail: CERF@vmbd.org
www.vmdb.org

Orthopedic Foundation for Animals (OFA)
2300 NE Nifong Blvd.
Columbus, MO 65201-3856
Telephone: (573) 442-0418
Fax: (573) 875-5073
E-Mail: ofa@offa.org
www.offa.org

US Food and Drug Administration Center for
Veterinary Medicine (CVM)
7519 Standish Place
HFV-12
Rockville, MD 20855-0001
Telephone: (240) 276-9300 or (888) INFO-FDA
http://www.fda.gov/cvm

Publications

Books

Anderson, Teoti. *The Super Simple Guide to Housetraining*. Neptune City: TFH Publications, 2004.

Anne, Jonna, with Mary Straus. *The Healthy Dog Cookbook: 50 Nutritious and Delicious Recipes Your Dog Will Love*. UK: Ivy Press Limited, 2008.

Dainty, Suellen. *50 Games to Play With Your Dog*. UK: Ivy Press Limited, 2007.

Morgan, Diane. *Good Dogkeeping*. Neptune City: TFH Publications, 2005.

Magazines

AKC Family Dog
American Kennel Club
260 Madison Avenue
New York, NY 10016
Telephone: (800) 490-5675
E-Mail: familydog@akc.org
www.akc.org/pubs/familydog

AKC Gazette
American Kennel Club
260 Madison Avenue
New York, NY 10016
Telephone: (800) 533-7323
E-Mail: gazette@akc.org
www.akc.org/pubs/gazette

Dog & Kennel
Pet Publishing, Inc.
7-L Dundas Circle
Greensboro, NC 27407
Telephone: (336) 292-4272
Fax: (336) 292-4272
E-Mail: info@petpublishing.com
www.dogandkennel.com

Dogs Monthly
Ascot House
High Street, Ascot,
Berkshire SL5 7JG
United Kingdom
Telephone: 0870 730 8433
Fax: 0870 730 8431
E-Mail: admin@rtc-associates.freeserve.co.uk
www.corsini.co.uk/dogsmonthly

Websites

Nylabone
www.nylabone.com

TFH Publications, Inc.
www.tfh.com

Index

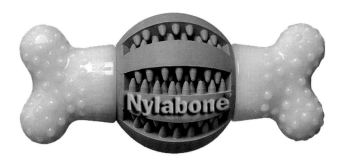

Photo Credits

Acknowledgments

Candace Mogavero, Faireland Kennel; Natalie Armitage, Overlook Kennel; Nancy K. Boyle, Heybern Showdogs; Robin Moser, Havanasilk Dogs Kennel; Lisa Finn; Wendy DeRouen; Suzanne McKay's *Colours of the Rainbow;* Billy Akins, Sandy Run Kennel; Havanese Club of America; American Kennel Club.

About the Author

Patricia B. McRae, Ph.D., is a retired professor and owner of Ahavapicaro Kennel. Coming from a farm and ranching tradition, but eventually needing her dogs to be smaller, she encountered and fell in love with the Havanese and Russian Tsvetnaya Bolonka breed. Established in 1997, Dr. McRae's kennel has fielded approximately 40 champions over the past 12 years. She co-founded and served as President of the Delaware Valley Havanese Club (DVHC), of which she remains a member, and is a member of the Havanese Club of America (HCA), where she has served on numerous committees.

NATURAL with added VITAMINS
Nutri Dent ®
Promotes Optimal Dental Health!

JOIN NOW
Club Nylabone
www.nylabone.com
Coupons!
Articles!
Exciting
Features!

360° Design
Cleaning Action!

Dogs Love'em!™
AVAILABLE IN MULTIPLE SIZES AND FLAVORS.

Nylabone®
Trusted For Over 40 Years

MADE IN THE USA